SONIC GRAPHICS

Seeing Sound

Matt Woolman

SONIC GRAPHICS

Seeing Sound

Thames & Hudson

CONTENTS

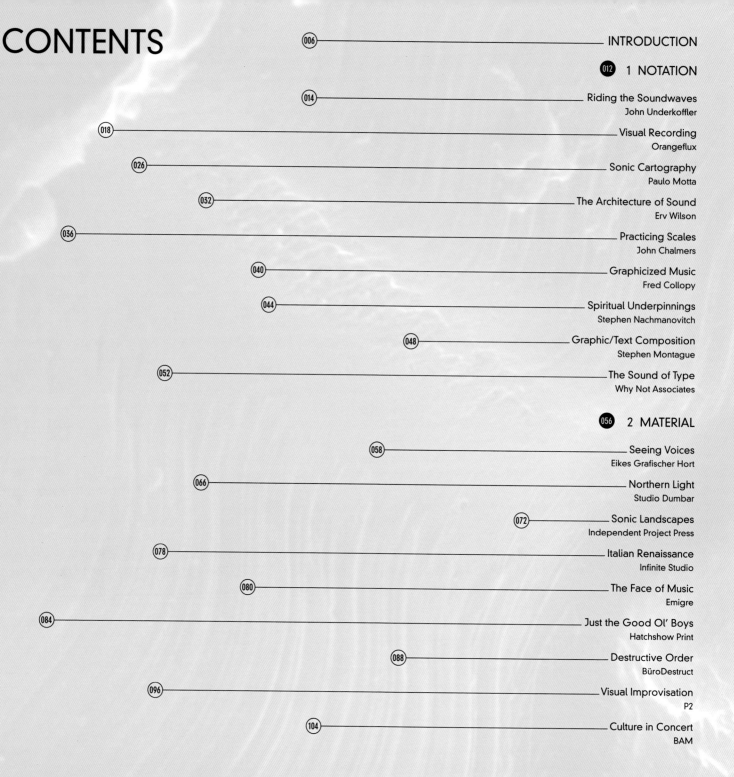

First published in the United Kingdom in 2000 by Thames & Hudson Ltd, 181A High Holborn, London WC1V 7QX

British Library Cataloguing-in-Publication Data
A catalogue record for this book is available from the British Library

ISBN 0-500-51021-0

Printed and bound in Hong Kong by C & C Offset

I would like to thank the following people for their consultation, generous assistance and contribution in the making of this book: First and foremost, all of the designers, artists, musicians and composers who took time out of their busy schedules to correspond, put forward their thoughts and ideas, collect and submit their work for publication; Center for Design Studies, Department of Communication Arts and Design, School of the Arts, Virginia Commonwealth University; John DeMao, Anne Graves, Dr. Richard Toscan, David Steadman, Jennifer Scheflen, Paul Caputo, Bob Kaputof, Ryan Lovelace, Nancy Nowacek, Jeff Bellantoni, Rupert, Calder, Ham, Ben and my friends and colleagues who spend their time playing and performing, listening and seeing. I extend a special thanks to Bruce Licher for

opening his record collection to me; Röby Clark for his insight, motivation and use of Cooper Black; and Charley Foley and Jarik van Sluijs for their thoughts on sampling as a sign system.

I owe a tremendous amount of gratitude to the following departments at Virginia Commonwealth University: School of the Arts Graphics Lab, particularly my colleague Jerry Bates and his committed staff: Kristina Adams, Shannon Conway, Linton Andrew, Jesse Tolj, Forrest Young. Thank you John Mehring for your 4 x 5 photography and occasional Black Sabbath flashback. Medical College of Virginia Media Production Services and Electron Microscopy Facility in the Department of Anatomy.

I give special recognition to Angeline Robertson who was at my side from the time this book was but a few thoughts on paper. Without her assistance, advice and support during the evolution of this project, Sonic Graphics / Seeing Sound would still be only a vision. Thank you.

This book was funded in part by a generous grant from the Qatar Foundation, School of the Arts, Virginia Commonwealth University. Additional (and generous) support was provided by the Center for Design Studies, Department of Communication Arts and Design, School of of the Arts, Virginia Commonwealth University.

For Ursula.

THE LANGUAGE OF MUSIC SEEN

Music is much more than the surface qualities as defined by a dictionary. It is about the movement of sounds through space and time. The ear is the primary receiver of music, but pulses, beats and vibrations are also felt by the sense of touch. The components of live performances—musicians, conductors, instruments, lights—offer a visual link to the expression of sound. Given these multisensory conditions, it is understandable why artists are so keen to explore the visual representation of this physically and spatially unconfined art. Gathered here is a collection of painters, composers, graphic designers, animators and others, who have advanced such exploration throughout the twentieth century. Using various methods, they share the common goal of visualizing sound.

Our journey begins with the fundamentals: notes. Just as letterforms represent the syntax of the spoken word, notational systems have evolved as universal symbols that express the entire form of the musical composition. In its function, conventional notation is almost too limited; the symbols remain the same, regardless of the intensity of the note or the instrument that is being played. The process of translating musical notation into sound involves both mechanics— the proper operation of the instrument—and personal interpretation, which is influenced by emotion and experience. Therefore, the same composition will often have as many sonic interpretations as there are musicians performing the piece.

In the history of Western music until around 1800, notation was used only as a means of putting notes into written form. After 1800, musical notation also encompassed the expression, or execution, of a composition. In England and the United States, <u>fasola</u> (shape notes, dating from the seventeenth century) attempted to give a visual quality to the note that was more closely aligned with its sound, and where the degrees of a scale were represented by syllables rather than letters. Another method, by Guido d'Arezzo, was illustrated by human hands that showed diagrams of chord arrangements on specific areas of the fingers.

It is interesting that the process of teaching music is the reverse of teaching reading. Speech comes before one learns how to read. Conversely, the music student is taught notation, specifically the diatonic scale, before performing a composition or playing an instrument.

The diatonic scale is considered to be the fundamental scale upon which Western music is based, and is produced by the white notes on a piano keyboard. The scale is defined in terms of eight notes that are separated by five whole tones and two semitones (intervals). It can start on any note, but the intervals remain in the same order. For example, C major scale is illustrated on the keyboard below, with "t" representing whole tones and "s" showing semitones. It also appears in conventional notation [below, bottom].

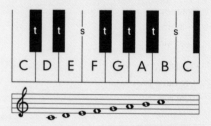

The diatonic scale repeats every eight notes (an octave), i.e., every seven intervals. Cumulative intervals are described by the range of notes they span; two intervals make up a third, three intervals make up a fourth, and so on.

Piano keyboards are tuned to what is called the twelve-note equal temperament system, with one black or white key for each semitone. As each tone comprises two semitones, this makes twelve equal intervals in an octave. These intervals are of the same frequency ratio or pitch difference, allowing the diatonic scale to start on any note, while the intervals remain constant.

PAUL KLEE: VISUAL COUNTERPOINT

Swiss abstract artist Paul Klee (1879–1940) was a trained musician and painter. Eighteenth-century music—particularly the principles of counterpoint—played a vital role in his teaching and theories. Counterpoint literally means, "note against note," or "melody against melody," and has taken many forms in the history of music, but can be summarized as harmonically oriented melodies.

In conventional musical notation, individual melodies (strings of single notes) constitute the horizontal elements on the musical stave, and the intervals between them are represented by the vertical elements. The twentieth century brought much experimentation in music, particularly the method of dissonant counterpoint, in which the linear relationship of melodies is emphasized and the vertical relationship is dissolved.

As a lecturer at the famed Bauhaus in Germany in the early 1920s, Klee often used counterpoint to illustrate such visual ideas as the relationship between one independent line of music and another. He also believed that art must possess universal, or absolute, content for it to have any value. Klee's works is non-representational in content, i.e., his means of expression are not based on narrative or symbolism. To achieve this, he looked toward the method of polyphony, the organization of multiple independent themes of pitch and time within a single musical composition. It was his painting entitled Ad Parnassum (1932) that Klee intended to be his ultimate polyphonic work, embodying his coding systems for counterpoint and polyphony. One of Klee's most significant works is Ancient Sound (1925), where he constructed a mosaic of rectangles and infused them with a harmonious spectrum of colors that correlate to musical scales.

VASILY KANDINSKY: SOUND, COLOR, COMPOSITION

Many studies have investigated the physical and psychological relationships of color and sound. Both the pitches of the musical scale and the colors of the optical spectrum are vibrations of specific frequencies. However, the correspondences between sound and colour are often determined by a given culture's accepted forms.

Russian abstract expressionist painter Vasily Kandinsky (1866–1944) also looked toward music for the roots of ultimate visual expression. After a trip to Paris in 1909, during which he saw the works of impressionist and fauve masters, Kandinsky launched a visual journey that brought his painting deep into the realm of abstraction. His first efforts involved loose, fluid forms infused with brilliant colors. By 1913, he began working on paintings that have become known as the first truly abstract works of modern art. Consisting of geometric elements with distinct outlines and sharp edges, these compositions were completely non-representational and "pure": they made no reference to the physical world. Instead, the inspiration for these works came from music, and Kandinsky employed such series titles as Compositions, Improvisations and Impressions.

The Compositions series is of particular interest, specifically Composition VIII (1923), which features circles, arcs, lines and other geometric configurations that resemble musical staves and notation. Another important work, Yellow–Red–Blue (1925), refers to the three primary colors, which dominate the canvas and are arranged in the same color sequence as the color scale. Kandinsky has published his theories in several essays and manuscripts.

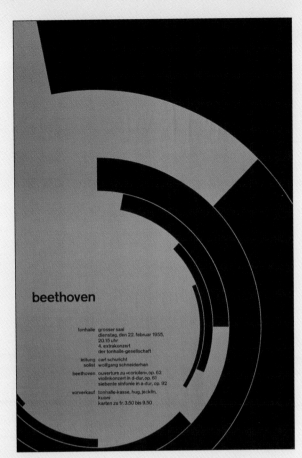

beethoven

tonhalle grosser saal
dienstag, den 22. februar 1955,
20.15 uhr
4. extrakonzert
der tonhalle-gesellschaft

leitung carl schuricht
solist wolfgang schneiderhan

beethoven ouverture zu «coriolan», op. 62
violinkonzert in d-dur, op. 61
siebente sinfonie in a-dur, op. 92

vorverkauf tonhalle-kasse, hug, jecklin,
kuoni
karten zu fr. 3.50 bis 9.50

Klee and Kandinsky have both made momentous developments on the painted canvas by looking at music and eternally framing the dynamics of sound. Other artists have used animation to visualize music as it unfolds over space and time. In conventional notation, the measures, staves and notes provide a linear diagram of musical events that move in horizontal and vertical motions. Similarly, frames of film also serve as an appropriate medium for the exploration of sound and image.

As early as 1920, German film-maker and painter Oskar Fischinger (1900–67) began an exploration of cinematic techniques in painting with a view to establishing a universal language of non-representational form, color and sound. This led to the production of a series of abstract films, also known as "absolute" films (films that do not follow a storyline or narrative). By the mid-1920s, Fischinger was using film to synchronize abstract imagery with popular music, in effect creating the first music videos. Each of these films is three minutes in length and includes almost five thousand drawings. Collectively titled Studies, the series was projected in movie theaters as advertisements for the music he visualized.

COMPLEX SIMPLICITY

Swiss graphic designer Josef Müller-Brockmann is known for his use of objective and constructivist graphic, and photo-graphic, elements that adhere to an underlying compositional grid.

Müller-Brockmann believes that music is the most abstract of the arts and argues that it can only be interpreted within the 2-D form of the poster. In 1951, he began a series of posters for the Zürich Tonhalle, a concert performance center. This legendary work used a compositional grid only as an alignment device for the typographic elements. The other geometric and organic forms departed from Müller-Brockmann's constructivist method and behaved in a free-flowing manner that directly expressed the time, space and motion of music.

The "Beethoven Poster" [left] was created in 1955 from a structure of concentric circles of varying diameters and line widths. The circles are fractured into arcs that seem to rotate at different pitches and rhythms to one another, evoking the musical genius of Ludwig van Beethoven (1770–1827).

ZÜRICH TONHALLE, concert poster, 1951
Müller-Brockmann created a sequence of floating abstract shapes to capture the musical structure of Prelude to the Afternoon of a Faun by Claude Debussy (1862–1918).

FONTANA MIX, 1958

"Fontana Mix" [far right] is a score by John Cage, made up of a series of translucent overlays. The performer creates the score by randomly layering selected sheets and, once set, it graphically plots when and where the instruments are played. Once this arrangement has been made, the performers must adhere to the score to avoid any improvisation or personal experience that might interfere with the performance.

CARTRIDGE MUSIC, 1960

This score [right], also by John Cage, consists of four transparent sheets and twenty opaque sheets, with both types of sheet showing dots, lines, numbers and circles. Each performer selects and arranges a combination of all the transparent sheets and one opaque sheet to form a single composition. "Cartridge Music" is timed by a stopwatch. Turntable needle cartridges and contact microphones are used as the instruments and are triggered according to a set of instructions that correlate with the lines and shapes in the score.

RICK GRIFFIN, Fillmore concert poster, 1968

Created by Rick Griffin, this poster [right] has become an icon for the visual language of San Francisco rock music in the 1960s. It illustrates a complete break from typography as a linear symbol system for communication. Griffin aimed to use the elements of communication—letters, numerals and other symbols—as works of art in themselves. Griffin's creative genius influenced the visual identities of many bands from the San Francisco area.

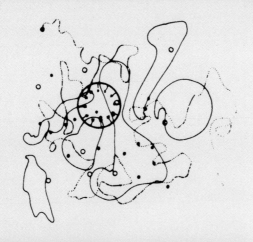

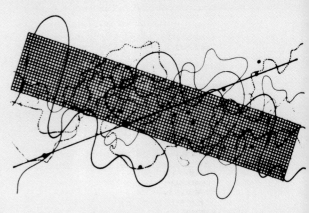

WES WILSON, Fillmore concert poster, 1967
Designer Wes Wilson uses color and extreme contrast in form and space to create an optic maze [above]. In many cases, the viewer literally has to be taught how to read these compositions.

Some of his later films, such as Allegretto (1936) and An Optical Poem (1937), caught the attention of Walt Disney, and Fischinger was contracted to animate several sequences for Disney's film Fantasia. However, he resigned from the project due to the many compromises imposed upon his ideas. Fischinger shifted his focus to painting, and produced work inspired by his filmic experimentation.

Released in 1940, Walt Disney's Fantasia was a breakthrough in animation with music, and it reached a wide film-going audience. Always pushing the boundaries of accepted techniques and effects,

Disney challenged his team to conceive a perfect synthesis of image and music. This was a departure from the previous method of animating outlined, flat characters to a background of bouncy, simple tunes that did little more than match the steps and limb motions, or indicate the contact of one object on another, for example, the clink as an iron pan hits a head. The animation in Fantasia was constructed with elaborate foreground and background matte paintings, overlaid cells, fades in and out between scenes and other effects that create an atmosphere that surrounds and envelops the characters and other animated elements. This was enhanced by fluid movements that were integrated (not just superimposed) with the musical compositions.

Fantasia could be called a visual record album, with Disney's animation synchronized to classical music performed by the Philadelphia Orchestra and conducted by Leopold Stokowski. In fact, it was the first movie to be released in stereophonic sound, christened "Fantasound" by Disney. For example, one sequence runs to The Sorcerer's Apprentice by Paul Dukas (1865–1935) and features the iconic Mickey Mouse as an aspiring magician named Yen Sid (Disney backward) who asserts his powers beyond the restrictions placed on him by his master. The Rite of Spring by Igor Stravinsky (1882–1971) plays to a dramatic story of evolution, from single-celled organisms to the extinction of the dinosaurs. Dance of the Hours by Amilcare Ponchielli (1834–86) led Disney to create a comic ballet performed by ostriches, hippos, elephants and alligators, while Night on Bare Mountain by Modeste Mussorgsky (1839–81) and Ave Maria by Franz Schubert (1797–1828) place the forces of darkness and light against one other.

The postwar decades of the 1950s and the 1960s also proceeded with considerable experimentation in musical composition and performance, abandoning structured rhythm, melody and instrumentation.

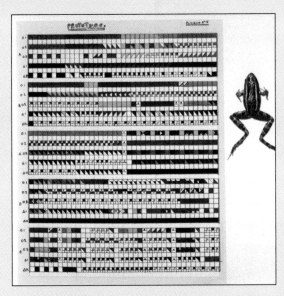

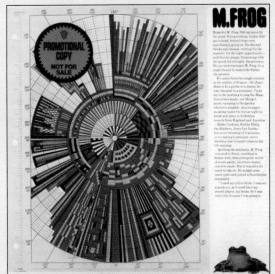

M.FROG, 1973
After a failed attempt to become a monk, M.Frog (Jean Yves Labat) returned to art school in Paris where he discovered "experimental" music. However, he thought that the musicians and their audience were too insular, so he ventured into the world of rock and roll music, where musicians were able to reach a much wider audience. He realized that rock musicians were actually able to make a living creating and performing their music. M.Frog's instrument of choice was the synthesizer and his music a combination of electronic and rock. He developed a new method of notation, based on color wavelengths and spectra, which featured on his first album [left]. The album cover was designed by the legendary New York graphic designer, Milton Glaser.

On his 1973 album cover M.Frog explains, "I have been trying to develop a notation for synthesizer music that works through colors . . . It isn't really necessary for rock and roll compositions, but you need it when you have a synthesizer interface where you might have five machines, a computer, and other things . . . It looks strange because most people are brought up on academic music notation, but electronic music requires a whole new system of notation just like the old Gregorian . . . I wanted to be very careful and not make [my album] so far out that no one could relate to it. But the unity of the album is in the color of the sound."

STARS OF THE LID & JON McCAFFERTY
Per Aspera Ad Astra, 1995
This CD project is a collaboration between Texas band Stars of the Lid and New York artist Jon McCafferty and synthesizes the packaging (visual) with the sounds to form a complete whole. The band recorded the CD in the dark, and a slide of McCafferty's painting (featured on the CD cover, left) was projected onto a screen. The musicians point out, "The merging of color and sound is something we've thought about quite often. Why should the visual artist be confined to the packaging while the "musician" is in charge of the rest—especially when both dimensions may reflect back onto each other. We wanted to craft a sound environment that is both true to Jon's painting as well as the larger New York context which envelops his work."

Composers sought new methods of conveying their musical ideas visually, which became collectively known as graphic scores. In some instances, they were intended to symbolize particular sounds and textures, while other systems were simply sets of instructions that often included chance operations during performance.

Led by the genius of John Cage (1912–92) and Karlheinz Stockhausen, such composers as Cornelius Cardew, La Monte Young, Morton Feldman, György Ligeti and Sylvano Bussotti have produced visually intriguing works that transcend their function as sonic maps for time and space to become artifacts of the synthesis of sound and image. The idea bound into many of Cage's scores is known as indeterminacy, whereby the outcome of a piece is unpredictable and decided by the composer and/or performer. Typically, the composer establishes a framework within which performers act. The one requirement of indeterminacy is that any and all actions and sounds occurring during the performance—even those of the audience—are allowed.

In the mid-1960s, San Francisco became the center for all things new, electric and wild in contemporary rock music. Within half a decade, one of the first musical subcultures arose, which has shaped the sight and sound of the music industry to this day. The genre of music known as "psychedelic" or "acid rock" encouraged a lively graphic language that found its way to album covers and concert posters. The artists hired by concert promoter Bill Graham used posters as the primary vehicle to communicate to an emerging hip teenage culture. The live performances at the legendary Fillmore, Winterland and Avalon concert halls often included dazzling light shows that painted the space and pulsed and vibrated to the music.

ANALOGUE TO DIGITAL

"What had been accomplished in music by the end of the eighteenth century has only begun in the fine arts. Mathematics and physics have given us a clue in the form of rules to be strictly observed or departed from, as the case may be."
Paul Klee, 1928

The link between math and music is an ancient one. The Pythagoreans—ancient mathematicians—formed this link when they used fractions to express the intervals within the octave range. The keyboard, particularly of the harpsichord, organ and piano, has been used throughout music history as a medium for coordinating the relationship of color and sound. However, the invention of the electronic synthesizer eliminated the twelve-note equal temperament and greatly expanded all musical exploration.

Controlled by computer processors, synthesizers can be programmed to a fraction of a second, which allows intervals smaller than semitones and known as microtones. Mexican composer Julián Carrillo was the first to divide the traditional musical scale in this manner and he invented special instruments for playing microtonal compositions. Several composers before Carrillo, however, were known to have used microtones unsystematically, namely Charles Ives and Béla Bartók.

The greatest advancement in electronic music can be attributed to Brian Eno in the 1970s. Eno studied conceptual painting and sound sculpture in England, and played synthesizers for the band Roxy Music. Experimentation resulted in the concept of "ambient music," which can best be described as the process of shifting the emphasis of the sound structure from a centralized source—the rhythmic interaction of percussion, guitar and bass—to a diffusion of sound from multiple sources—natural, mechanical and man-made. There is not a distinct structure and the listener is not focused on the "object" of the sound, but rather is lead through a sonic landscape, picking up aural fragments along the journey. In 1977, Eno released the album Before and After Science, which has become an icon in the postmodern approach to musical composition.

The genre of music known as "techno" describes the current phase of electronic music, which began in the 1990s from the foundations laid by Eno. Every genre of music is associated with a visual language, normally portrayed in the faces of the musicians, the packaging of their recordings and even the fans and venues for live performance. Techno has few or no recognizable faces. Instead, listeners identify with names, for example, Scanner, Spooky, Autechre, Orbital and The Crystal Method.

Today's designers of CDs, vinyls, mini-vinyls, mini-discs and even the posters and flyers that publicize raves and other music–dance events, are challenged to visualize the language of music. This language often features saturated fluorescent colors, metallic and other specialized printing inks, collage, montage, sans serif typefaces and geometric graphic elements arranged on underlying grid structures.

AN ALCHEMY OF SOUND AND IMAGE
Digital technologies have reduced all recording and playback media used in the reproduction of musical notes and visual marks to the same molecular properties: the bit. A single bit, short for "binary digit," translates into a simple yes/no command, and is read by the computer in terms of 1 (positive, or on) and 0 (negative, or off). The bit is the smallest element of information that a computer processes. Combinations of two or more bits form a code that allows the computer to present information in ways that

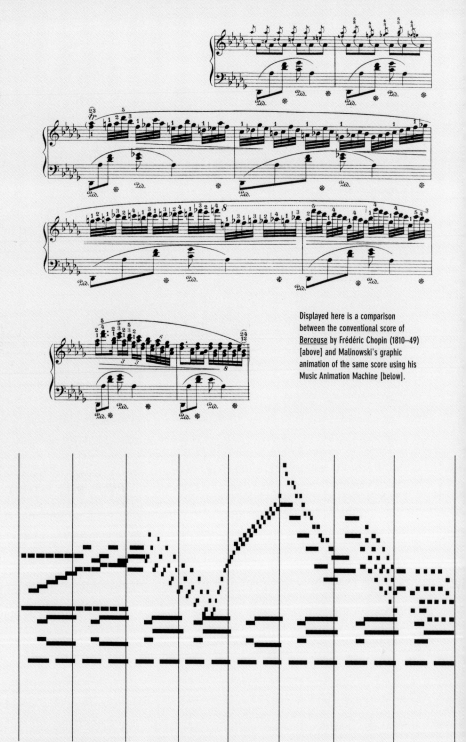

Displayed here is a comparison between the conventional score of Berceuse by Frédéric Chopin (1810–49) [above] and Malinowski's graphic animation of the same score using his Music Animation Machine [below].

MUSIC ANIMATION MACHINE
This piece of software by Stephen Malinowski makes animated graphical scores of musical performances. The scores are specifically designed to be viewed on videotape or computer screen while listening to the music. Stephen Malinowski's inspiration comes from the visual theories of Paul Klee, and a desire to extract conventional musical scores from their static page-frames. They contain much of the information found in a conventional score, but display it in a way that can be understood intuitively by anyone, including children.

Each note is represented by a colored bar and different colors denote different instruments or voices, thematic material or tonality (the color has been removed from the above score, to make the graphic forms clearer). The bars scroll across the screen from right to left as the piece plays, and each bar brightens as its note sounds to provide a visual marker for the viewer. The vertical position of the bar corresponds to the pitch: higher notes are higher on the screen, lower notes are lower. The horizontal position indicates the note's timing in relation to the other notes.

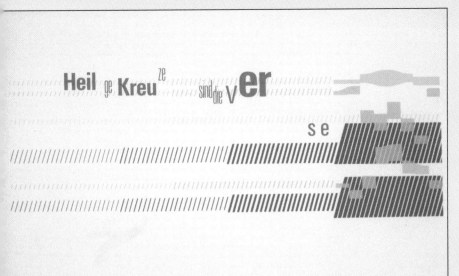

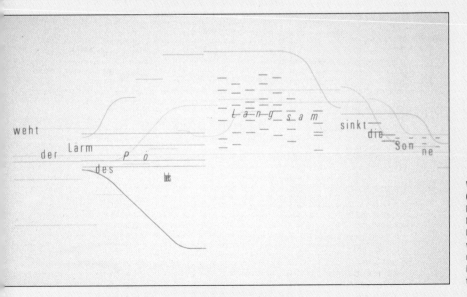

humans understand: text, image, sound. Thus it seems a natural evolution to merge all three methods of communication.

<u>Sonic Graphics / Seeing Sound</u> discovers a place where sound is seen and image is heard. The collection of work on these pages is too vast and too varied to define a new visual field or "movement." It is, therefore, best compared to a record collection that has evolved over time, and includes a variety of musical genres: classical, jazz, blues, folk, country, rock, pop, new age, urban, world and electronic. A well-chosen record collection embodies not only the recorded music, but also the passage of time, travels through space and place, and evocations of thoughts and memories both personal and universal.

As with a record collection, this book is not finite: it is only a pause. Musical boundaries are constantly changing with the pace of developments in digital technology. The underlying goal of <u>Sonic Graphics / Seeing Sound</u> is to expose the reader to new methods of thinking about the relationship between sound and image. It encourages the reader to analyze the factors of form, function, technology and context in visual music and, its inversion, music visualization. Some of the specimens presented on the following pages are intriguingly complex, others are frighteningly simple. Whether you are a musician, designer, artist, computer programmer, music fan, or all of the above, I hope after you close this book you are left with some resonance and inspiration of what lies ahead for our human senses in this increasingly digitized world.

VISUAL SOUND, 1978
Graphic designer and design professor Frank Armstrong has found connections between aural and visual fields in a language that visually defines music variables. Armstrong writes, "A parallel relationship exists between the interaction of visual forms (including typographic letterforms and other elements) and the interaction of sounds within their respective mutually exclusive spatial fields." He has employed this language system in a series of three visual translations [left] of a portion of <u>Pierrot Lunaire</u> by Arnold Schönberg (1874–1951).

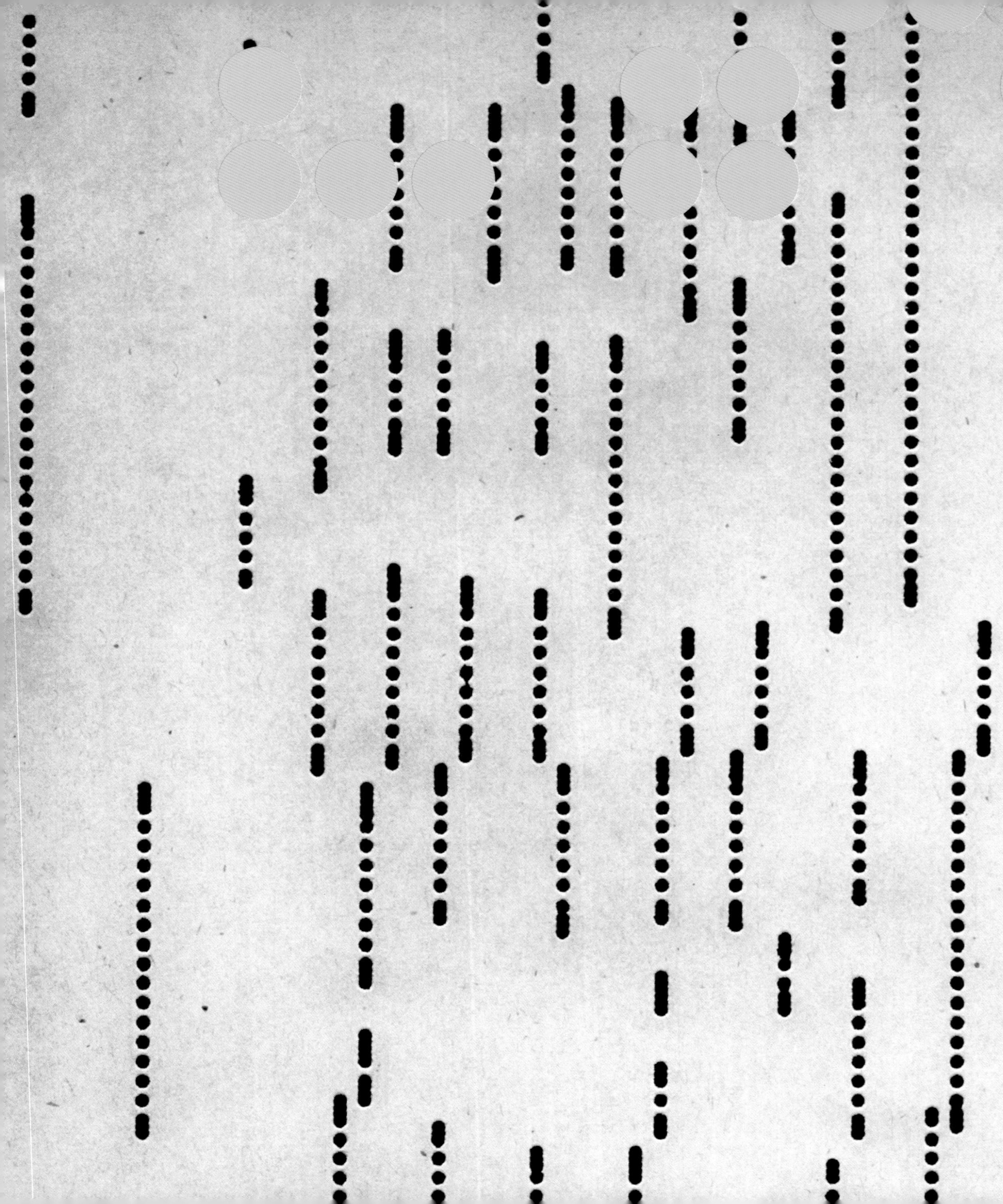

YOU

WANT

I

MORE

1
NOTATION

Humans cultivate the ability to create and respond to rhythm before they are confronted with the complexities of written and spoken language. The pulses, beats and vibrations of structured rhythm and melody—music—represent a language that is naturally and universally felt by individuals, no matter what their geographic origin. But music, as both a creative aural phenomena and an industry, is no longer driven by sound alone. Digital technologies allow a synthesis of the seemingly disparate elements of sound and language to produce a heightened sense, awareness and understanding of both. This section presents coding and symbol systems—the architecture—used in converting music to image and image to music.

RIDING THE SOUNDWAVES

John Underkoffler completed his PhD at the MIT Media Lab in 1999. For some of the fifteen years during which he served at this New England brain trust, Underkoffler researched optics and holography under the MIT Spatial Imaging Group's HoloVideo program. He contributed to the invention of several new kinds of holographic stereogram that improved visual sophistication and created the world's first fully shaded, electronically reproduced, real-time hologram. Subsequently, his interest turned to the production of novel interaction techniques. Underkoffler's later dissertation resulted in the I/O Bulb and the Luminous Room, techniques that allow the transformation of interior architectural surfaces into sites for information display and interaction. These systems have demonstrated their usefulness in such fields as optics, hydrodynamics and urban design.

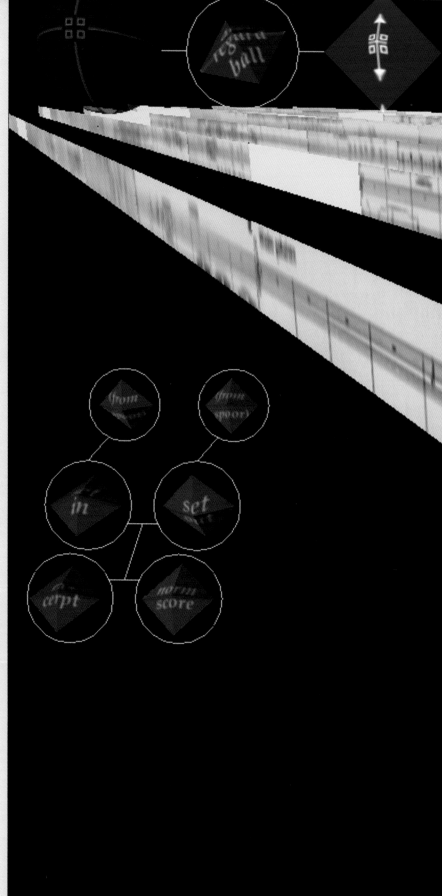

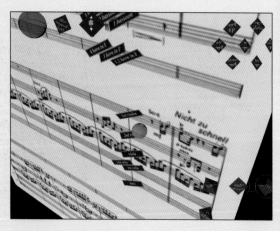

The UnderScore project was an attempt to construct a coherent and functional 3-D information space that was both easy to apprehend and to navigate. It was, in a way, a reaction to much of the other "3-D spaces" work of the day, which only superficially engaged the possibilities of the extra dimension as a novelty to be exploited without having to depart from two-dimensional design strategies.

The real provenance of UnderScore was as a paean to musical typography, which Underkoffler had long admired: a beautiful, compact, tremendously well-designed notation system that had evolved over half a millennium. Despite this crisp communicative efficiency, it can be very difficult—even for someone with formal musical training—to follow an unfamiliar orchestral score as the music unfolds. Underkoffler wanted to build a system that would use real musical typography—instead of trying to re-engineer it—and one that would provide an environment for synchronized reading and listening, making it impossible to lose one's place.

UnderScore presents an audio performance of a piece together with the annotated scans of the actual sheet music. The navigator soars above the typeset score, described by one viewer as "a sort of flight simulator for music." The viewer follows a bouncing "now ball," whose position shows the aural performance point and the particular instrument being tracked, and whose jaunty hopping tracks the meter and evolving tempo of the piece.

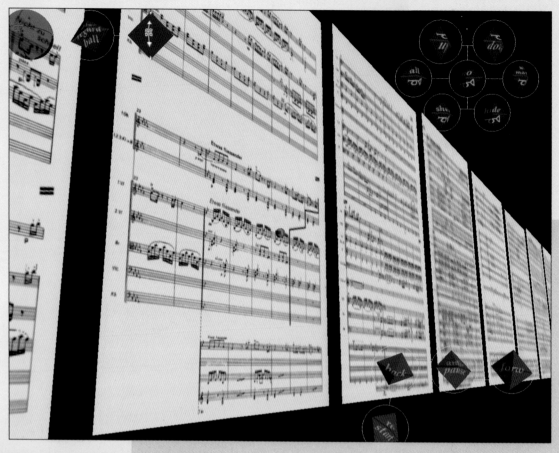

Various functions are provided by floating control clusters, each imbued with gentle motions in accordance with the project's general design principle of constant dynamism. The controls are truly three-dimensional and inhabit the same space as the musical information whose exploration they assist; in some cases, the controls emit tools that fly to and alight on the score, providing a kind of in-situ manipulation.

Simple controls allow the navigator to pause momentarily, or start again from the beginning, with the audio performance following along in lock step. Other controls permit the smooth adjustment of the view forward or backward through the score, up or down the stack of staves, and so on.

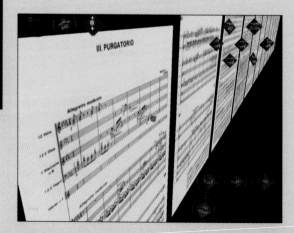

Markers can be deposited at interesting locations throughout the score and can be revisited. More complex operations indicate the beginning and end of a particular passage along with a subset of the full instrumentation. UnderScore can rearrange the score to produce an excerpt, cutting strips instrument by instrument from the original. It then lies them end to end to provide notation without page boundaries.

It also distributes these ribbons of continuous visual music in 3-D digital space, so that the staves for each instrument are stacked back to front, instead of top to bottom. Another function allows the music to be disassembled glyph by glyph. As the performance progresses, notes that have been played are disposed of ecologically, lifting off the page and flying into the ether.

VISUAL RECORDING

Orangeflux is an independent graphic label, a description chosen by the founders to reflect both their interest in music and their goal to broaden the scope of graphic design to include many different forms. The members create work that questions and challenges the definition of graphic design; shifting design as a service to design as a product. They feel graphic design should inspire and entertain, not just sell.

The Orangeflux label was initially founded in 1996 to release digital typefaces.
As Orangeflux expands the definition of design, the "label" can be seen as an
umbrella under which many different processes take place, from traditional
graphic design to furniture and clothing design. They never want to limit themselves.
Orangeflux rejoices in its ability to create things that display its graphic fingerprint
and to contribute to the dialog of graphic design and music today.

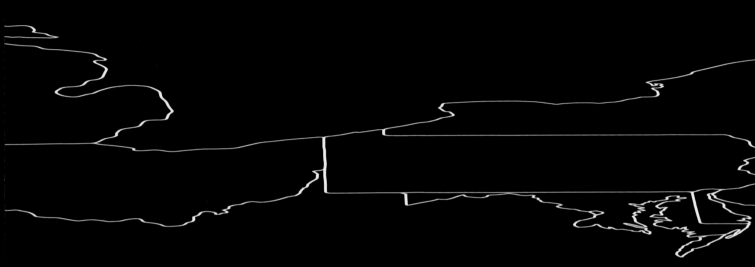

Orangeflux began with a love of typography. The founding members spent every spare hour creating typefaces: characters would grow into words and then into paragraphs. Each face produced its own unique voice.

The one discouraging factor of typeface design was the end use. These extremely expressive fonts were being forced into traditional roles (brochures, ads, etc.). It was like having a favorite tune transformed into a jingle to sell the latest shoe or car; somehow, it cheapened and destroyed the integrity of the original art. Orangeflux was interested in design as a product in itself.

They set out to create an alternative to the classic use of a typeface. They began to think musically and to

consider composing with fonts. Individual characters could be played like notes, enhancing lyrical content. The results would be processed with the eyes, not the ears. Orangeflux coined the term "visual recording" to describe the first release, "Rust Belt."

In order to integrate further design with music, "Rust Belt" was packaged in a 12" x 12" (30.5 x 30.5 cm)

letterpressed record sleeve. The designers sent out a few promotional copies and, to their delight, they found that some recipients put it in a stack of records for future listening—the packaging idea was working!

Orangeflux's working method for "Rust Belt" resembled the recording of music, with the output being a visual product. Graphically, the idea was to communicate Chicago's industrial and immigrant history by mixing craft with technology. Ink pens, xerox machines and computers became instruments of choice.

Writing lyrics was a tough but enjoyable task. The designers studied such great songwriters as Bob Dylan and Lou Reed to gain insight and inspiration. It was a learning experience that taught them to appreciate the art of songwriting, as much as creating type made them marvel at master typographers.

After finishing the lyrics, the designers began composing. The characters were to be the notes and voice of the compositions. Visually, they tried to underscore concepts like rhythm, harmony, contrast

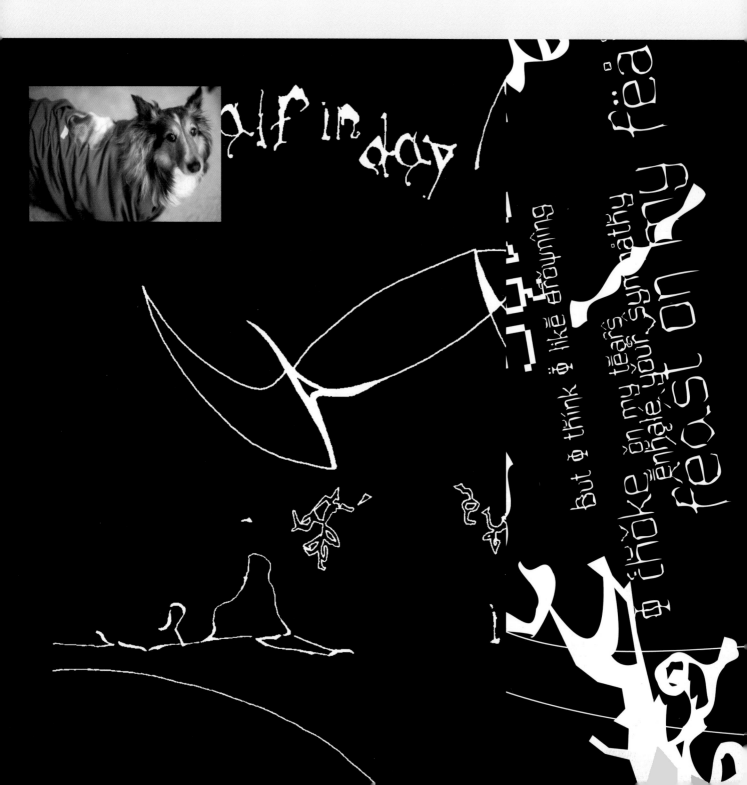

and repetition. They were also conscious of the mood of each song; one might be a soothing ballad and the next a thrashing scream.

Orangeflux found it a challenge to make design more intuitive and improvisational. Music can change in an instant, design is generally more static and planned. The designers wanted to bring the emotion, spontaneity and flexibility of music to design. In

trying to achieve these goals, they experimented with techniques like xeroxing, cutting and pasting, computer-generated art and hand drawing. They also found that readability, or lack thereof, could add depth to the tracks, mimicking a vocalist's octave range.

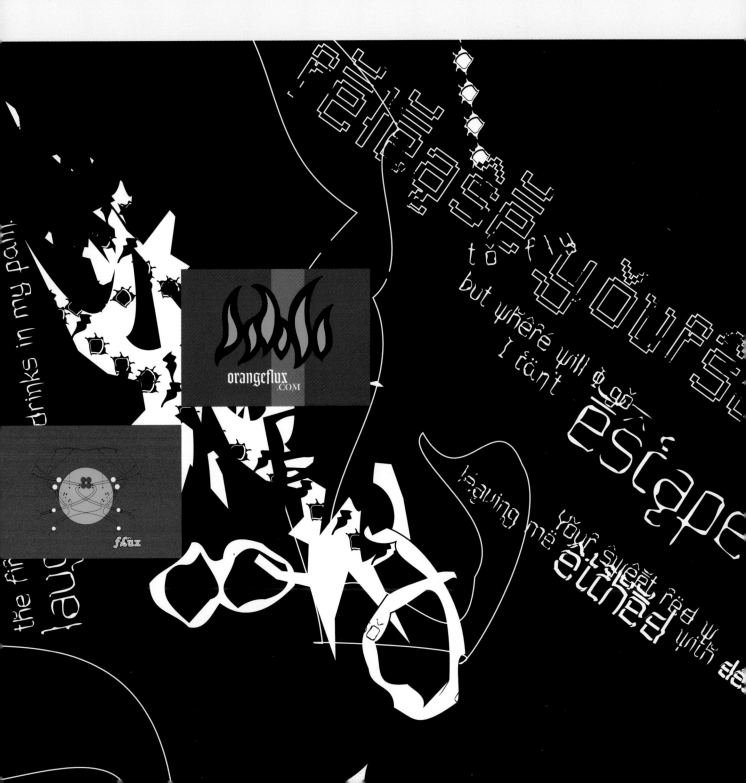

As soon as the actual piece was complete, attention turned to the marketing side of the product. Orangeflux had a simple plan. Like an "indie" band, they began to develop a brand identity: T-shirts, posters, stickers, etc., all became part of the total package. Magazine articles gave them much-needed exposure, and their website addressed inquiries and orders and posted submissions of original art.

The overall aim behind "Rust Belt" was to create an artifact, an item that was collectible instead of disposable. As with an album or book, it was designed to be taken off the shelf from time to time, each time revealing something new.

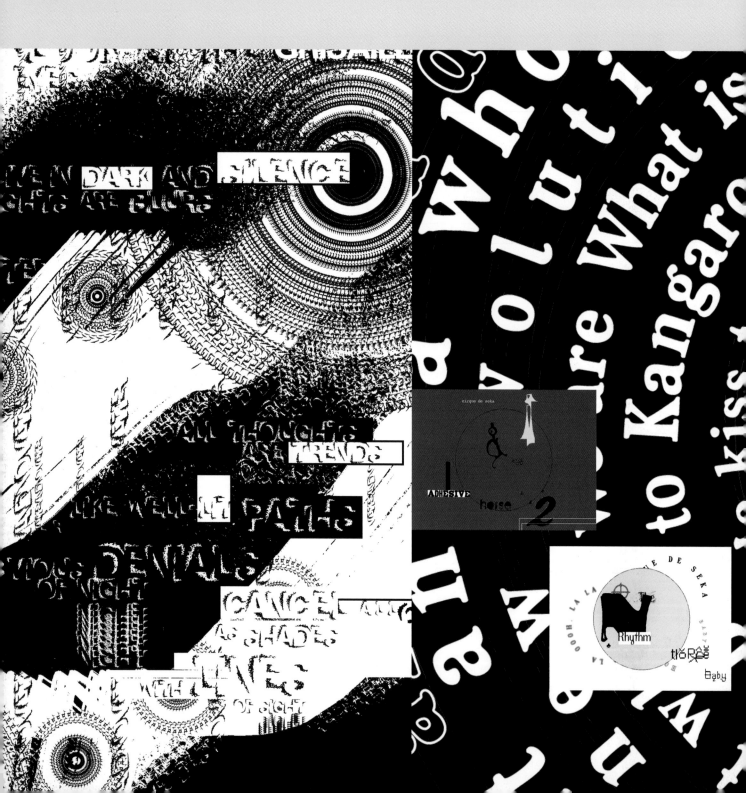

When the first release was on the market, Orangeflux refocused on another project: "Love Horse," which featured on a CD-ROM called The Codex Series. This time, the designers integrated even further music with design in an interactive piece [see color insets below].

Somewhere between a game and a song, "Love Horse" allowed the viewer to navigate through three verses, adding sound and graphics through a "boom box" control panel. Working digitally offered such powerful features as audio and motion, but it was missing the tactile element of print.

SONIC CARTOGRAPHY

Paulo Motta's research involves the history, comparison and aesthetics of contemporary music, and he is particularly interested in integrating the compositional process with new technological means. In the early 1980s, the Brazilian native was one of the founding members of Uavisiliu, a multimedia experimental group that combined music, dance, visual arts and poetry in performances to mark the centenary of the city of Volta Redonda in Brazil. In 1992 Motta created the Atlas Musicalis Project that studies the writing of music as it relates to cartography, a prominent theme in his work. Motta is now analyzing electroacoustic compositional processes.

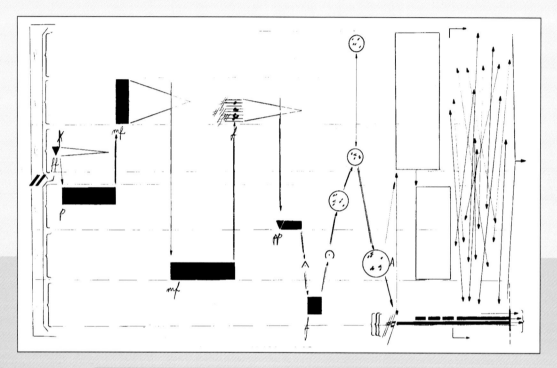

CHANCE MUSIC

The term "chance music" is often used synonymously with indeterminate music. It refers to any music where there is a chance or unpredictable result, which can be initiated by the composer, performer or even the audience.

Chance music is the opposite of improvisation. Improvisation allows the performers to draw upon previously stored experiences and information and to contribute, with a certain amount of freedom, to the performance as a whole. In this example, the control involves a set of parameters that defines the style of the performance. Indeterminate music requires the sounds and other actions to happen as they happen, regardless of framework or result.

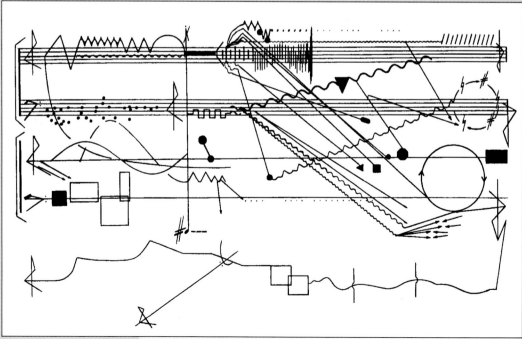

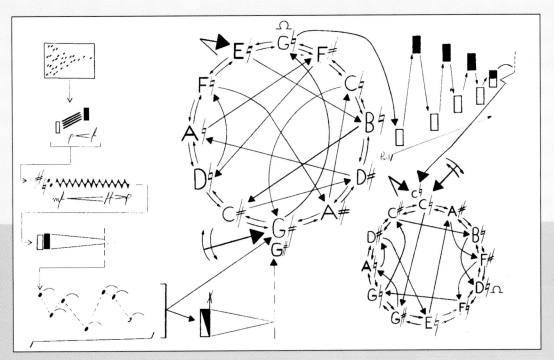

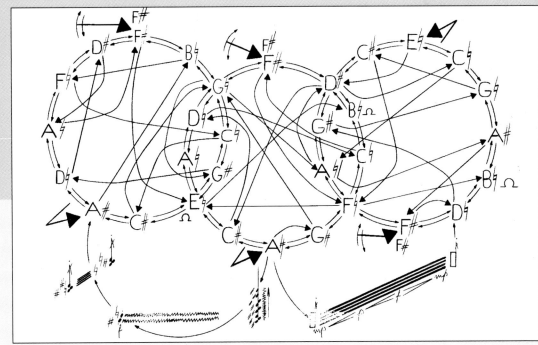

THE ANAMORFOSES I SERIES, 1993
An eleven-page composition for an indeterminate number of instruments. Motta's graphic scores serve as sonic maps for the performers to follow. The elements—staves, clefs, notes, rests—look familiar, but the compositions are purposely structured to permit chance actions and unpredictable outcomes.

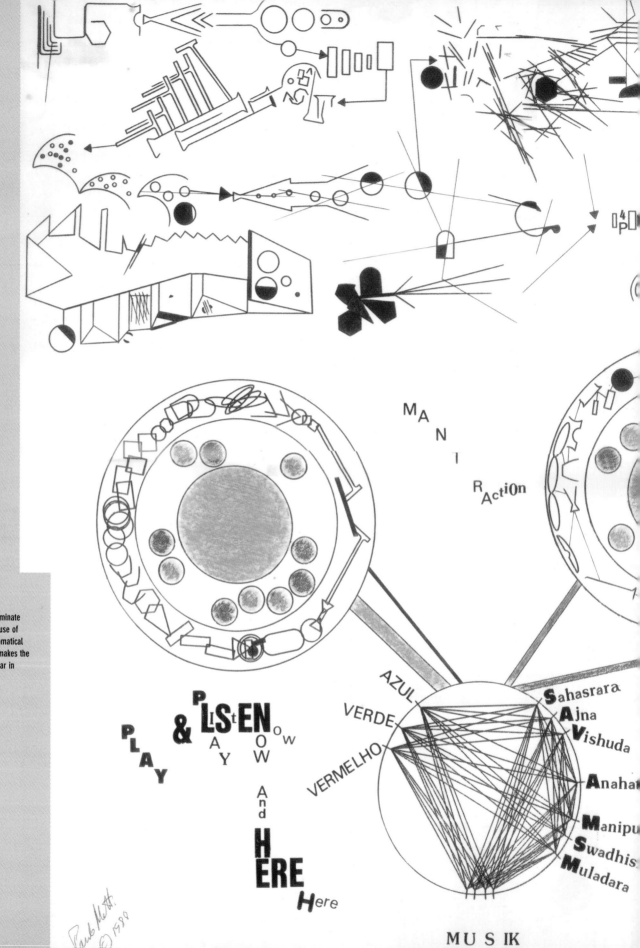

MEDITATION SOUNDS, 1988
A composition for an indeterminate number of instruments. The use of color and the strong diagrammatical sense of separate locations makes the reference to map-making clear in Motta's musical notation.

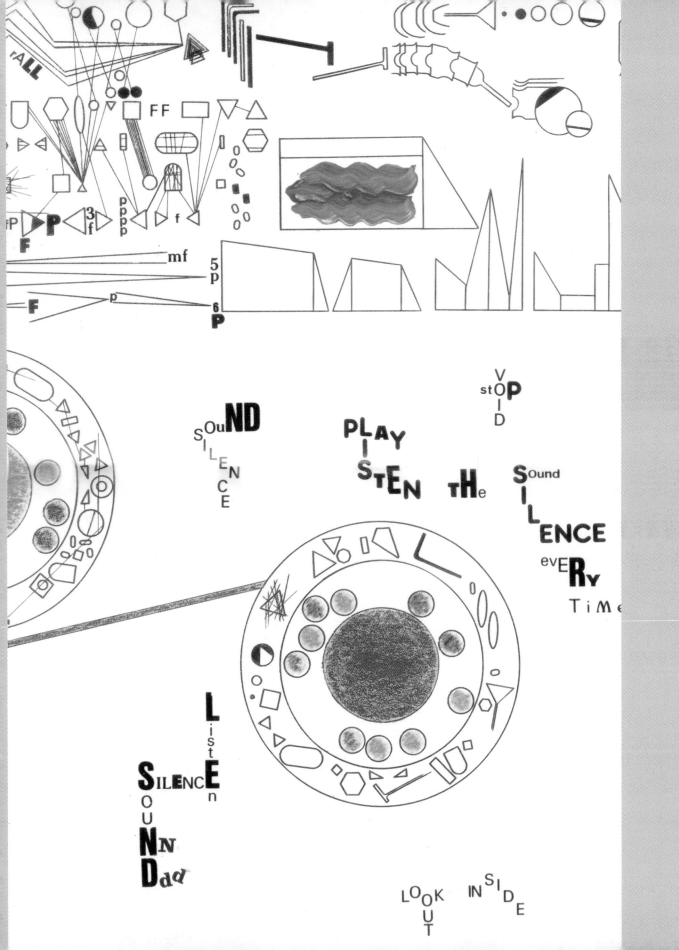

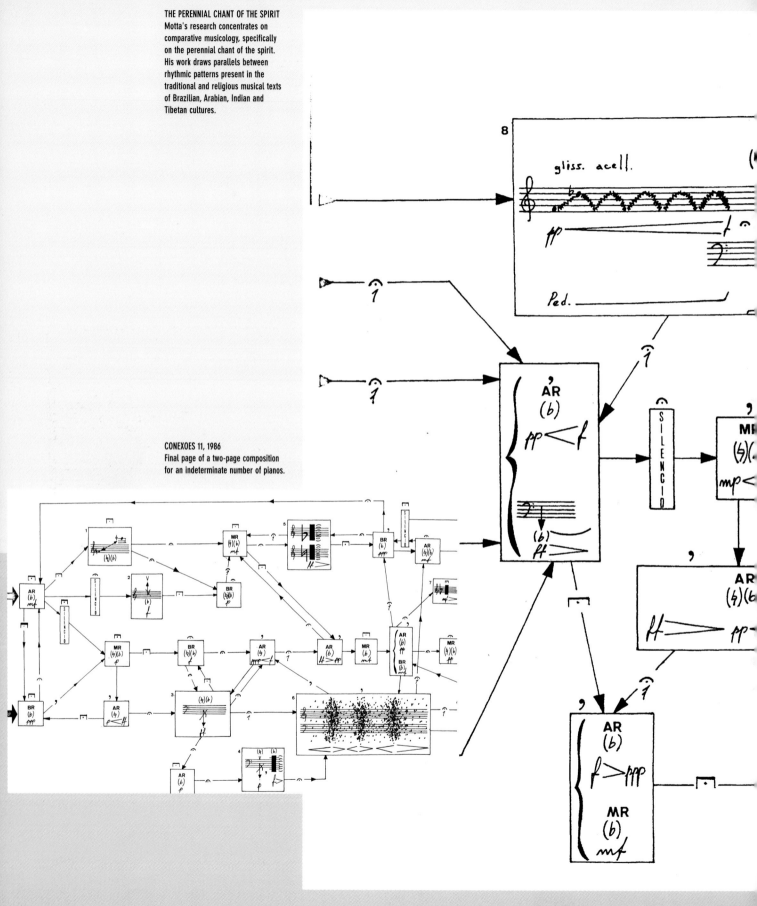

THE PERENNIAL CHANT OF THE SPIRIT
Motta's research concentrates on comparative musicology, specifically on the perennial chant of the spirit. His work draws parallels between rhythmic patterns present in the traditional and religious musical texts of Brazilian, Arabian, Indian and Tibetan cultures.

CONEXOES 11, 1986
Final page of a two-page composition for an indeterminate number of pianos.

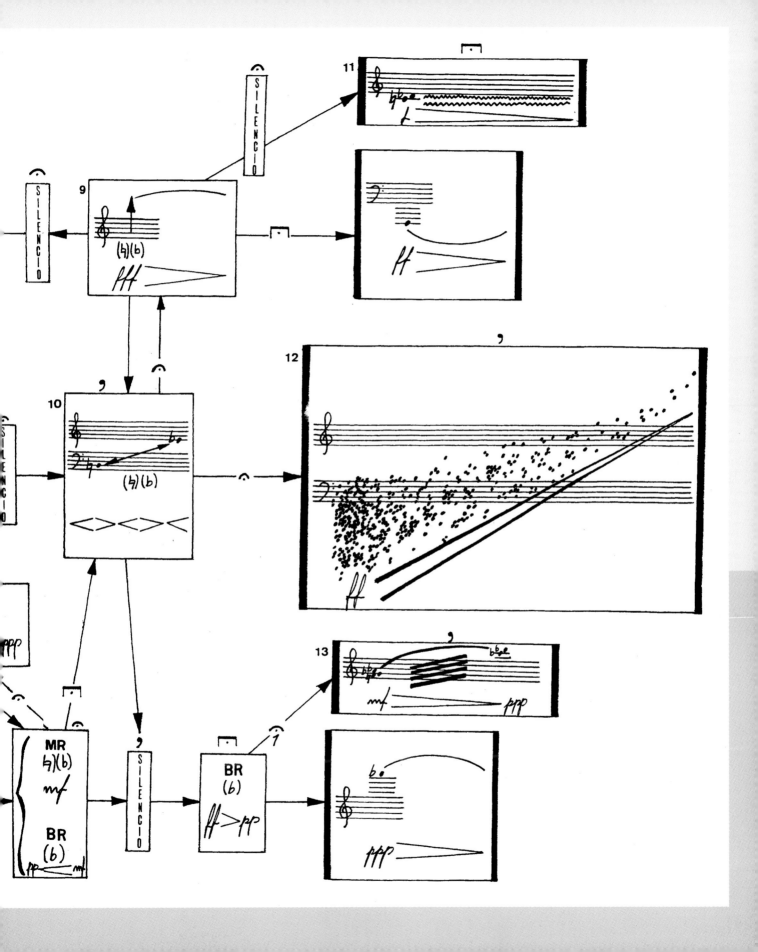

THE ARCHITECTURE OF SOUND

A number of composers and theorists employ tonal lattices—visual frameworks of intersecting lines and points—to depict harmonic relationships between the notes of the diverse set of musical scales they use. These scales are conceived in terms of what is called just intonation, a system of tuning based on notes whose frequencies are related by ratios of small integers. In general, every prime factor defines a separate harmonic function and is assigned to a unique graphic axis. Erv Wilson's experiments with mathematical music began in the mid-1960s. His research involves visually mapping mathematical translations of musical principles, predominately pitch and tonality.

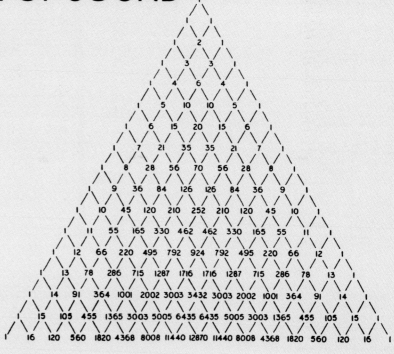

PASCAL'S TRIANGLE

PASCAL'S TRIANGLE

Wilson's visual mapping began with a search for a musical use for Blaise Pascal's triangle, known as "Pascal's triangle." Pascal, a French philosopher and mathematician, is credited for the invention of an adding machine and the development of the modern theory of probability. Pascal's triangle is essentially a visual adding machine. The top of the triangle contains the number 1, which is added to itself in the next row down in the triangle to produce 2 in the third row. One is then added to 2 to produce 3 in the next row, and so on down the triangle until five-digit numbers are achieved.

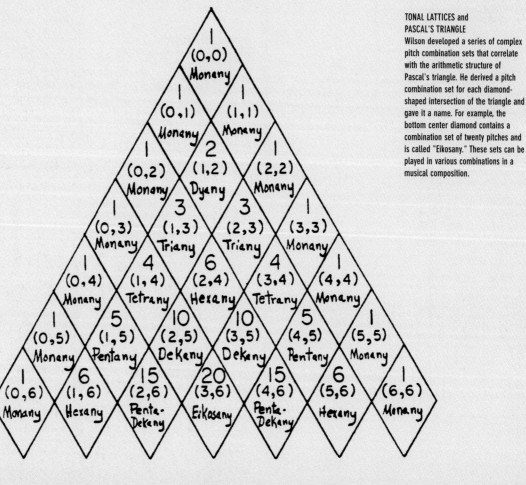

TONAL LATTICES and PASCAL'S TRIANGLE

Wilson developed a series of complex pitch combination sets that correlate with the arithmetic structure of Pascal's triangle. He derived a pitch combination set for each diamond-shaped intersection of the triangle and gave it a name. For example, the bottom center diamond contains a combination set of twenty pitches and is called "Eikosany." These sets can be played in various combinations in a musical composition.

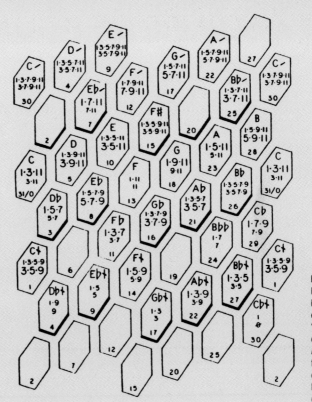

KEYBOARD LAYOUTS
Wilson took his research further and came up with individual diagrams that represented each pitch combination set. This was the basis for a keyboard program that could embody all the pitch sets. The sets are taken from the bottom row of the Pascal triangle formation.

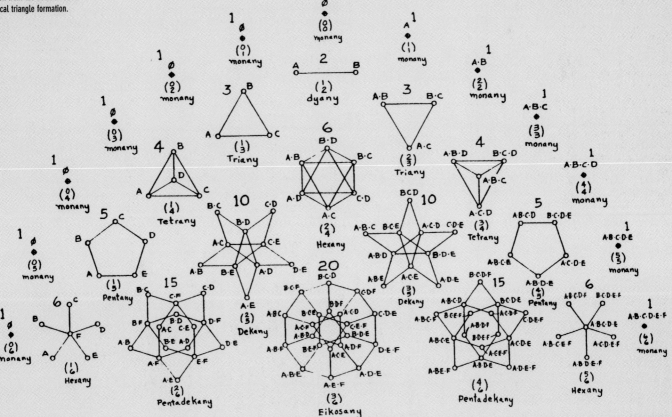

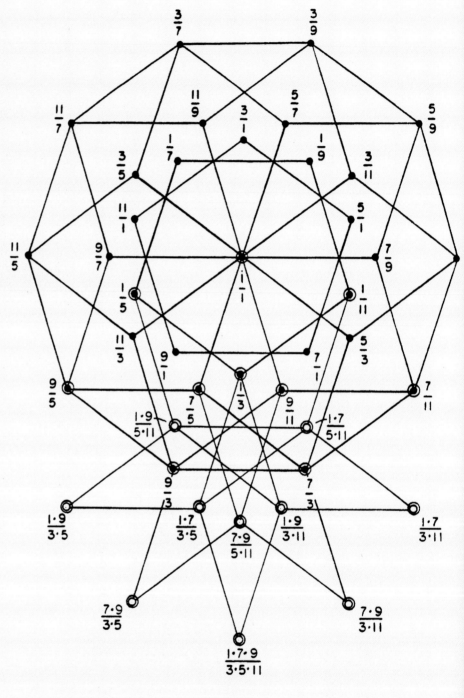

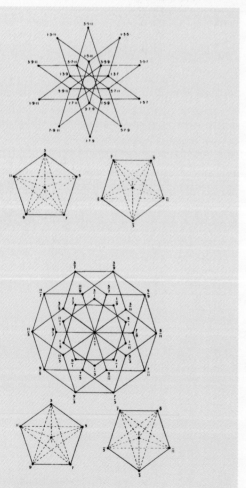

EIKOSANY [top] and DIAMOND, 1969

Intersection of DIAMOND and EIKOSANY, 1989

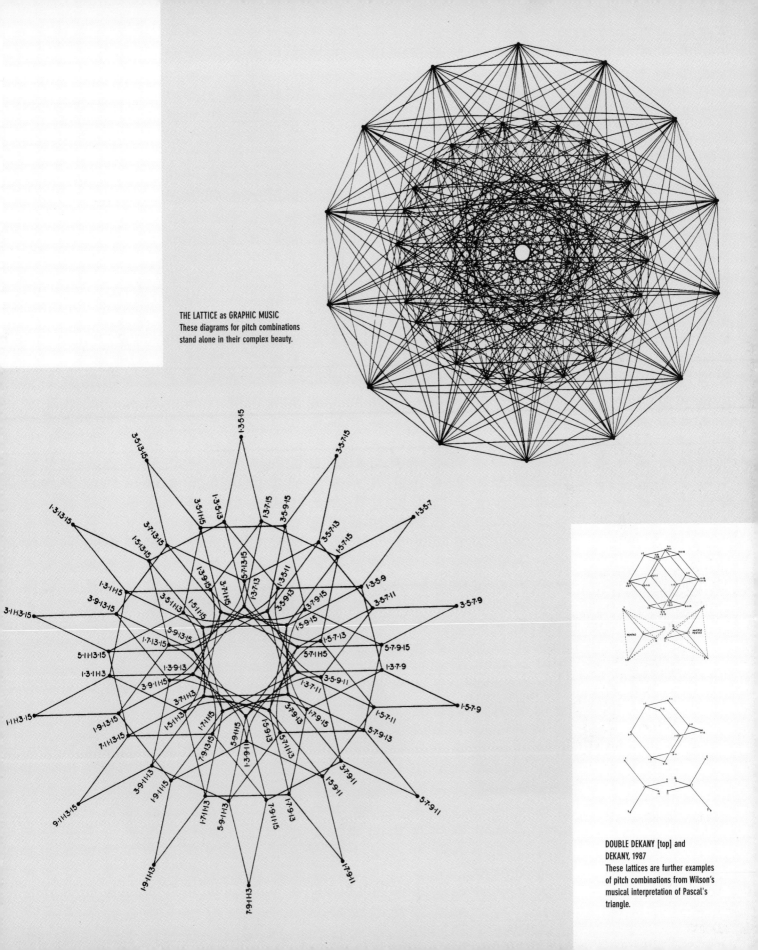

THE LATTICE as GRAPHIC MUSIC
These diagrams for pitch combinations stand alone in their complex beauty.

DOUBLE DEKANY [top] and DEKANY, 1987
These lattices are further examples of pitch combinations from Wilson's musical interpretation of Pascal's triangle.

PRACTICING SCALES

Although a biologist by training, John Chalmers is a music theorist by avocation, having become fascinated by the possibilities of non-traditional music after hearing Julián Carrillo's pioneering microtonal work <u>Preludio a Cristobal Colon</u>. In the mid-1970s he began publishing <u>Xenharmonikon</u>, an informal journal of microtonal music.

Over the years Chalmers has found that various lattice and linear diagrams are useful for revealing the harmonic and melodic properties of new scales. He has discovered that lattice diagrams illustrate the harmonic relationships between notes but obscure the melodic pattern of the scale. Conversely, linear or spiral diagrams and pie plots express the melodic character but conceal the harmonic pattern. Consequently, Chalmers has selected to work on several modes of graphic illustration on the basis of their aesthetic impact or novelty. He has been influenced by the work of Erv Wilson, some of whose beautifully hand-drawn lattices he has programmed so that numerous new scales can be portrayed easily, quickly and in color. Chalmers has also developed new space-saving spiral representations of the scales that convey both melodic and harmonic information within the same design.

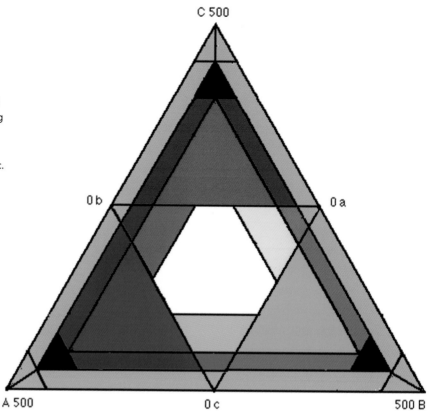

POLYCHROME TRIANGULAR GRAPH
Different types of seven-tone scales that are generated by taking two identical tetrachords—a group of four notes from a twelve-tone row—and a whole tone, are shown as variously colored zones of the underlying triangular grid. The white semi-regular hexagon in the center maps the extent of diatonic scales (standard Western musical scales composed of tones and semitones).

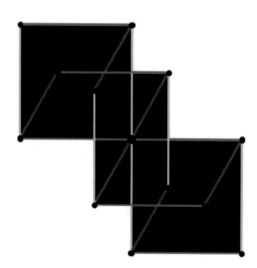

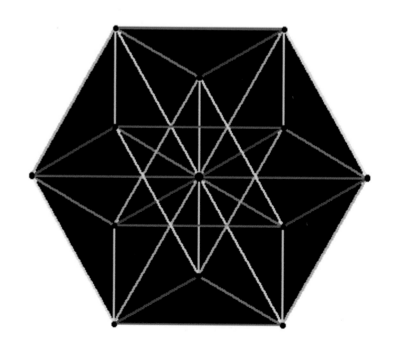

BLACK BACKGROUND TONALITY DIAMONDS
The "7-Limit Incipient Tonality Diamond" is a musical construct consisting of a dominant 7th chord in just intonation built on each of the notes of the octave inversion of the prime form. The concept of the Tonality Diamond was independently discovered by Augusto Novarro of Mexico and Harry Partch of the US. "7-Limit" means that the highest prime number used to define pitch relations is seven.

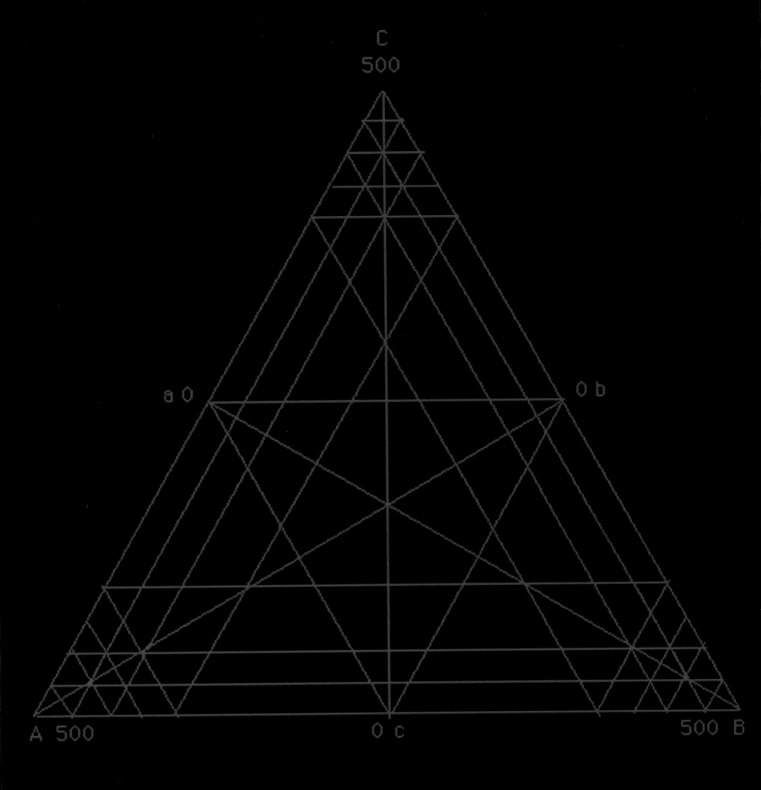

RED TRIANGULAR GRAPH
This appeared on the cover of Chalmers's book <u>Divisions of the Tetrachord</u> (Frog Peak Music, 1993), designed by Carter Scholz. It represents what Chalmers calls "complete tetrachordal space" and shows all arrangements of the three intervals of all tetrachords. Chalmers adapted this diagram from those used by physical chemists to describe the properties of three component mixtures, because the three subintervals of the tetrachord must add up to a perfect fourth.

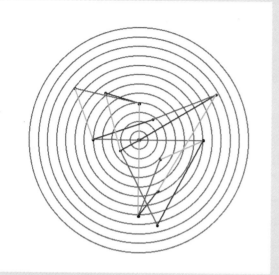

PLANETARY PLOT
The unusual appearance of this plot
was devised by Chalmers after
discussions with Joe Monzo as a
means of simultaneously indicating
both the sizes of scalar intervals and
their harmonic relationships. The
concentric circles represent the
familiar twelve-tone chromatic scale
and are 100 cents apart.

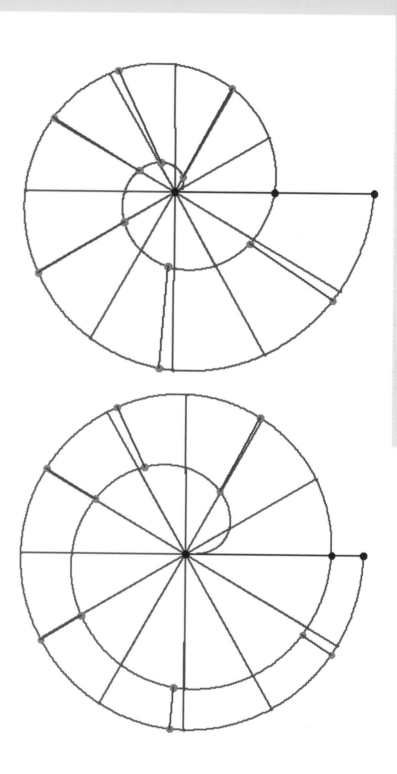

MAJOR SCALE SPIRAL PLOTS
Two octaves of the major scale tuned
as a mode of Ptolemy's Intense Diatonic
genus are shown on two different
spiral plots.

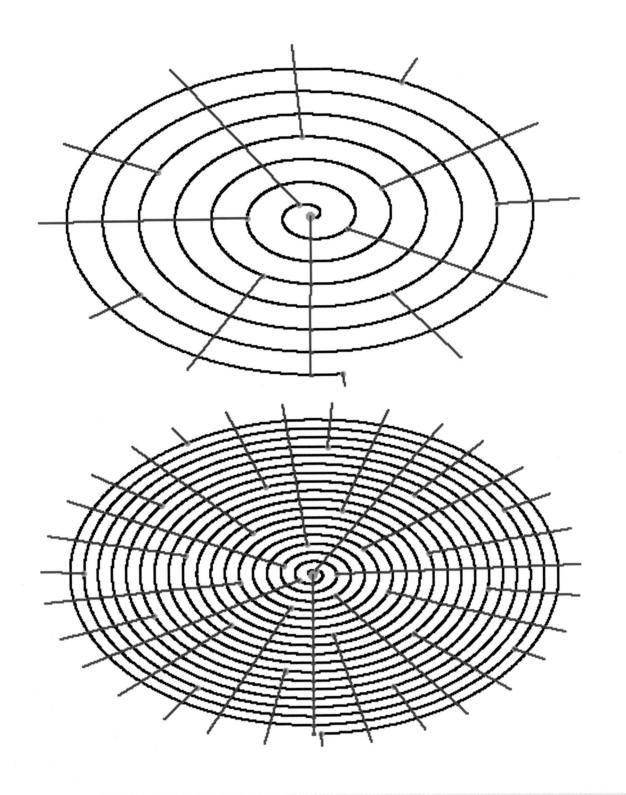

ELLIPTICAL SPIRAL PLOTS
The two cycles form the basis of the
twelve-tone and thirty-one-tone equal
temperaments. The red line links the
start of the cycle to its octave and the
blue lines connect the octaves of each
generated note.

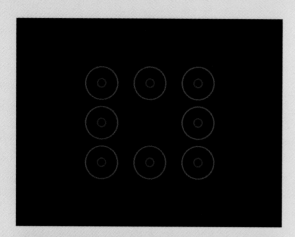

GRAPHICIZED MUSIC

For centuries artists have wanted to infuse their work with rhythm and other musical qualities. Artists at the Bauhaus combined visuals with musical performance and absolute (abstract or non-narrative) film-makers created rhythmic compositions for film in the US. The availability of computers has made dynamic graphic work more feasible, often driven by ideas from such artists as Vasily Kandinsky, Paul Klee, Morgan Russell and Karl Gerstner.

Fred Collopy, a member of the information systems faculty at the Weatherhead School of Management at Case Western Reserve University in Cleveland, Ohio, has embraced this history and invented Imager, a software instrument that allows artists to play with imagery just as musicians play with sounds. Imager uses MIDI controllers to compose colors, lines, planes and rhythms. Collopy is also a visiting scientist at IBM's Thomas J Watson Research Center.

UNAUTHORIZED DUETS
Collopy creates what he terms "Lumia;" graphic sequences that are animated by a music CD placed in the computer. Presented on these pages are lumia that are part of a series Collopy calls "Unauthorized Duets" because they were created as interpretations of previously existing music, rather than as collaborations with the musicians. The visual portion of the duets can be downloaded on to any computer.

BLUE MOVES
Duration: 5.28 minutes
Lisa Lehman and Fred Collopy created this interpretation of the Eileen Ivers's composition "Blue Groove" over several months. The piece starts with eight pairs of concentric circles and an occasional light-blue "visitor" circle in the center of the configuration. While the animated orbs change in size, shape, color and movement throughout the piece, they survive until the end when dramatic cymbal crashes scatter most of them. Ivers refers to the piece as a "studio jam." Collopy and Lehman try to capture some of the spirit of jamming in the movement of the circles.

Music: Eileen Ivers, <u>Wild Blue</u> (Green Linnet Records)

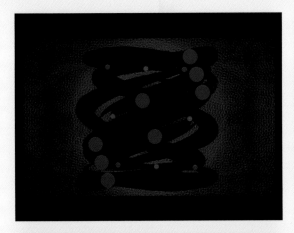

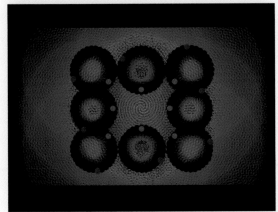

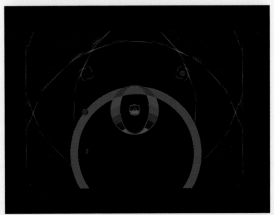

THE INFLUENCE OF COLOR WHEELS
Since Sir Isaac Newton, scientists and artists have devised color wheels. Several early color wheels, including that of the influential nineteenth-century color theorist Ogden Rood, placed yellow complementary to blue. On many modern color circles, for example, those of Johannes Itten and Faber Birren, orange complements blue. This piece opens with pairs of blue and yellow concentric circles. On a cymbal crash, one of the first dramatic moments in the piece, the yellow circles become orange.

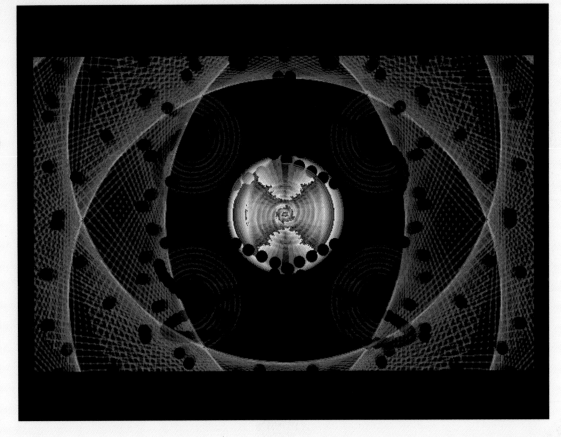

weDDDing

Duration: 5.04 minutes

Collopy had been graphically animating polygons that leave behind traces of their movement, and had become interested in their relationship with tight rhythm tracking in electronic soundwaves. This led him to recall a David Bowie composition, "The Wedding." The bells at the opening of the piece, the strong base line and the many small percussive accents, all lent themselves to the texture he wanted for a lumia.

Collopy was in the early stages of composing the piece when the computer graphics researcher and author Cliff Pickover showed him a pair of intriguing 3-D glasses. The glasses worked by shifting the perceptual plane of blue light back, and that of red light forward. Collopy employed this method to create three distinct planes through the middle section of his piece. The glasses were also responsive to the amount of saturation in a color, and in the last part of the piece Collopy used this effect to make the concentric polygon structure appear to change shape. This particular 3-D technology permitted him to create a piece that plays well with or without the glasses.

Throughout the piece, movements and changes are initiated by percussive details in the music. Each polygon leaves its first position in response to the same musical trigger. Similarly, later in the piece each floating line becomes yellow and starts its journey to the center of the screen in response to the same repeated musical event. When the last line joins the group, there is a tension-release moment in which the collection of lines is transformed into the nested polygon structure. Throughout the piece the rhythm of the music is reflected in the images.

Music: David Bowie, <u>Black Tie/White Noise</u> (Savage Records)

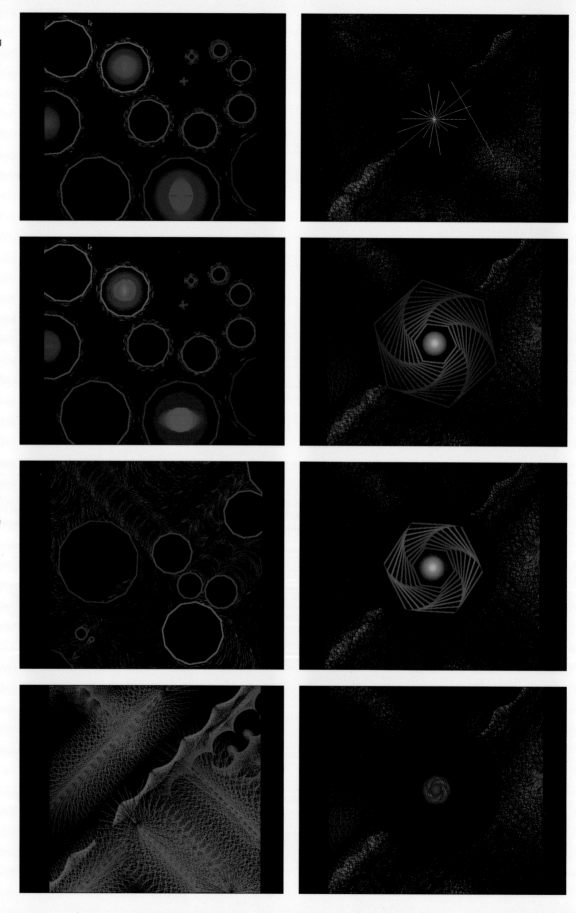

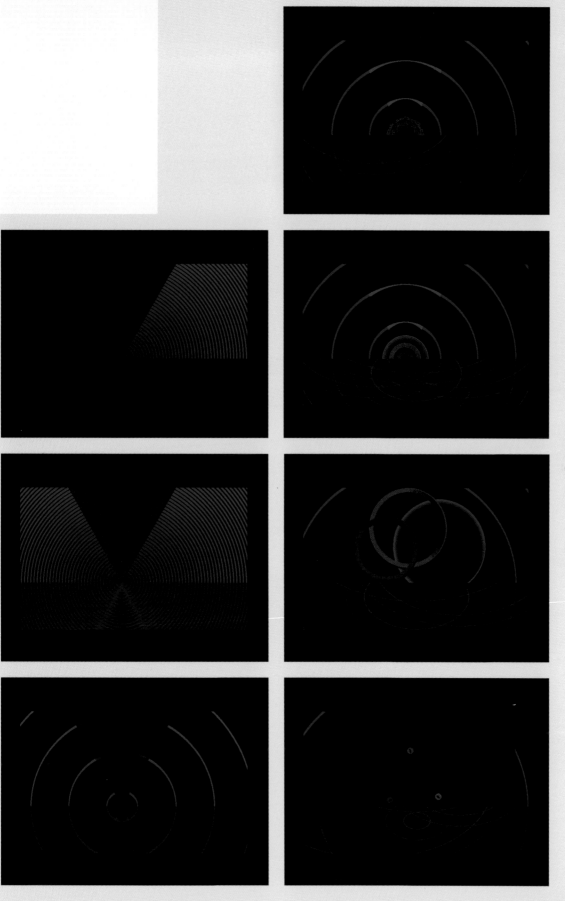

FILMS FOR MUSIC
Duration: 3.15 minutes
The 1978 Brian Eno album <u>Music for Films</u> contains a collection of richly textured short pieces, which Collopy enjoyed experimenting with. He came across the album when he was developing the first version of Imager for Apple II computers. Collopy was also taken with the idea of turning Eno's album title on its head.

At the time Collopy was investigating chromatic reflection and wavelike movements and wanted to create an improvisational piece. He played Eno's album and one particular cut seemed to fit perfectly with the fairly dark and spare images. Only later, when Collopy was preparing notes to accompany the piece, did he learn that the cut was entitled "Slow Water."

The viewing frame for this piece is horizontally divided into two sections. The graphic elements in each section are cropped to achieve the effect of moving into and emanating from one another.

No lighting or texture models are used, just simple 2-D plotting. The shadowing effects are achieved by slight variations in color value and in the width and shape of the pen line. The reflection effects in the lower section of the viewing frame are created by running two versions of the same object in each frame, with the lower section being slightly skewed. The images in the lower section have darker color values than those in the top to further emphasize the reflective effect on a digital surface.

Music: Brian Eno, <u>Music for Films</u>
(EG Records)

SPIRITUAL UNDERPINNINGS

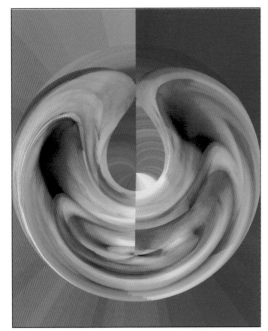

Stephen Nachmanovitch is an author, musician, computer artist and educator. Born in 1950 he studied at the universities of Harvard and California, where he earned a PhD in the history of consciousness for his investigation of William Blake. He has taught and lectured widely in the US and abroad on creativity and the spiritual underpinnings of art.

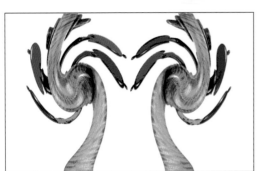

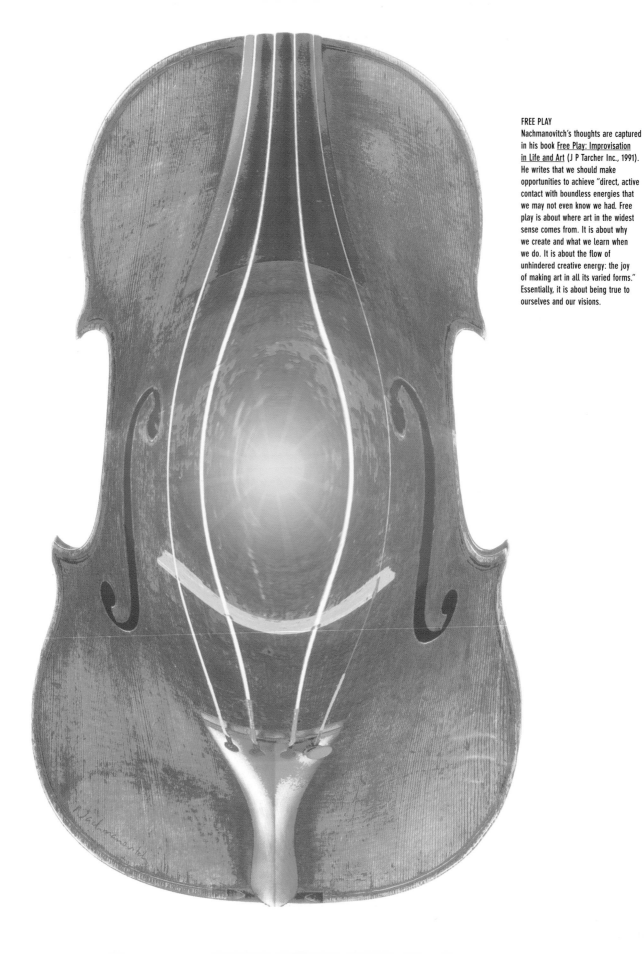

FREE PLAY
Nachmanovitch's thoughts are captured in his book <u>Free Play: Improvisation in Life and Art</u> (J P Tarcher Inc., 1991). He writes that we should make opportunities to achieve "direct, active contact with boundless energies that we may not even know we had. Free play is about where art in the widest sense comes from. It is about why we create and what we learn when we do. It is about the flow of unhindered creative energy: the joy of making art in all its varied forms." Essentially, it is about being true to ourselves and our visions.

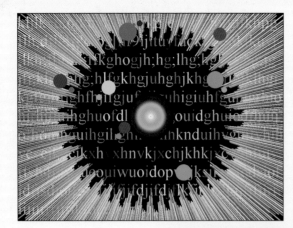
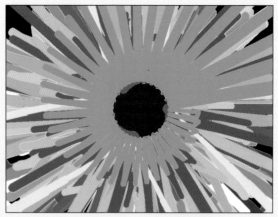
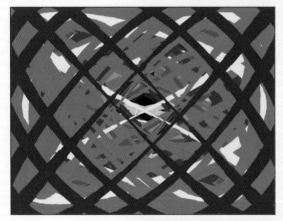
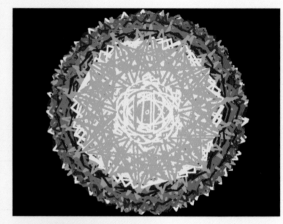

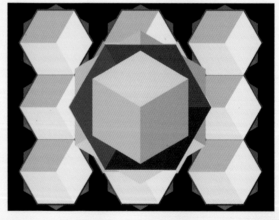

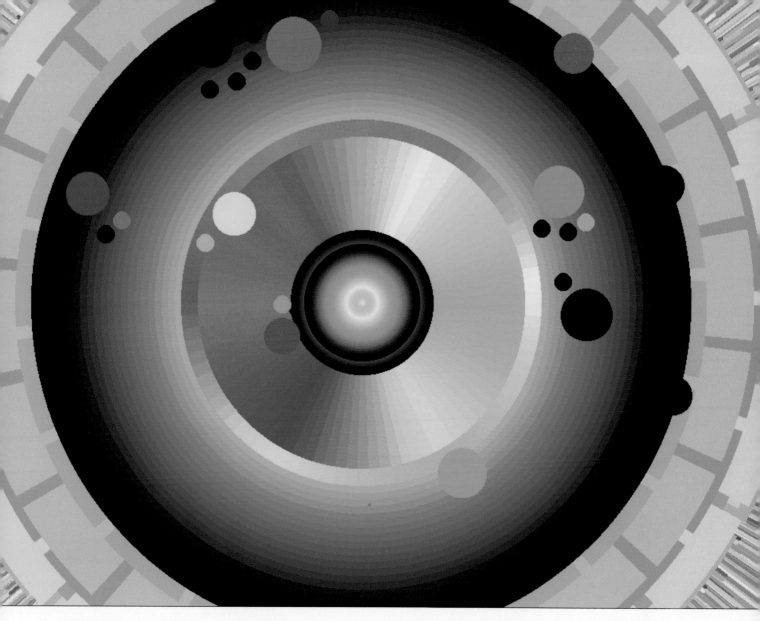

VISUAL MUSIC TONE PAINTER

This is an exciting program that converts signals from synthesizers or other MIDI instruments (manipulated by the player) into a visual display in real time. It merges sound, light and touch, bringing music to life by allowing the user to paint with sound. The player creates mandalas of light and sound by choosing from a palette of geometric shapes, ranging from simple circles, polygons, spirals and waves to more complex structures, such as letterforms, 3-D spinning cubes and such other curve-based forms as epitrochoids and Lissajous figures. These all respond to pitch, but also to the subtle nuances of finger pressure and release.

The musical dynamics are reflected through visual transformations in size, movement, hue, saturation and value. As the music develops, seemingly simple geometries build into moiré patterns, strobing and other multilayered effects.

Visual Music Tone Painter arose out of twenty years of work in the field of visual music and synesthesia. Two previous software incarnations were Zmusic and Mind's Moiré, which received their first public showing in 1986 and 1990, respectively.

GRAPHIC/TEXT COMPOSITION

American composer Stephen Montague has worked around the world and his compositions have been performed in such international venues as Hong Kong, Singapore, Paris, London and Warsaw. As a pianist, he has played at New York City's Carnegie Hall, Queen Elizabeth Hall in London and the Centre Pompidou in Paris. In addition to his numerous achievements as a composer and performer in the US and Europe, Montague has produced what he calls "graphic/text" scores since 1975. These scores can be read like poetry, or performed like a musical composition.

A
dan
cer lies
motionles
s in a darke
ned space with
a single spot light
directly over head.
As slowly as is physic
ally possible begins to ri
se from the position of rep
ose. The audience should har
dly be able to perceive moveme
net. Over a long period of time s
he finally arrives at a standing pos
ition then- slowly raises her head......
A shattering electronic chord in at least
four loudspeakers suddenly destroys t
he silence. The spot light is immediat
ely extinguished. The dancer leaves
the space when the light goes out
and the loud chord decrescend
os almost imperceptibly by
means of filters and a gr
adual reduction of lev
el until there is com
plete silence. Th
e silence is the
end of the
work.

▽

LARGO CON MOTO, 1976
Dancer, spotlight, 4-channel electronic sounds.

"Largo Con Moto" was the first in the series of graphic/text scores. Each work is a set of instructions that appears in words arranged in a visual layout, which shows the sonic shape of the piece and how it is to be performed. In this work, the dancer or performer lies motionless on the floor of a darkened hall with a spotlight overhead. Almost imperceptibly the dancer begins the long and difficult task of eventually standing upright.

A group of people (performers and/
or audience) sit in a comfortable position,
preferably on the floor, stage or the ground, legs
crossed and relaxed. With eyes closed and after a few
minutes of silent meditation, they begin to softly hum their
lowest comfortable sound or note. [This is recorded on a reel to
reel tape recorder in either two or four channels at 19cm/s (7.5 ips)
or 38cm/s (15ips)]. They gradually explore their own body's fundamental
sounds and resonance using overtones/multiphonics and various other vocal
devices. At some point the recording is gradually faded out, the spool reversed
so that it plays backwards and the speed changed to half of its original: 19cm/s now
at 9.5cm for example. The reversed tape plays along with the live vocalists until the taped
tape runs out. The piece ends sometime after the tape finishes and the last person finishes
vocalizing…chaaaaaaaaaaaaaaannnnnnnnnnnnnnntiiiiiiiiiiiiiiiiiiiiiiiiiiiiiiiiiiiiiiiiiiiiiiiiiiinnnnnnnnnng.

SOTTO VOCE, 1976
A group of vocalists chanting, reel-to-reel tape recorder.

"Sotto Voce" was inspired by some of the extended vocal techniques and multi-phonics executed by composer and performer Dary John Mizelle at the InterMuse Festival in Tampa, Florida in 1976. In Montague's work the vocalists improvise using whatever resonance their bodies will yield. The result is recorded on a reel-to-reel tape deck as they perform and is then played backward at half speed, dropping their vocal pitches to pedal tones an octave lower.

FOUR GROUPS OF PERFORMERS PLAYING
WINE GLASSES IN FOUR DIFFERENT AR
EAS OF A DARKENED, BUT CANDLE
LIT SPACE GRADUALLY CHANGE
THE CHORD BY DRINKING
OR FILLING THE WINE
GLASSES UNTIL
A PER
FECT
U
N
I
S
O
N
IS
FOU
ND BY ALL FOUR
CHORUSES OF WINE GLASSES.

Four groups of performers playing
wine glasses in four different ar
eas of a darkened, but candle
lit space gradually change
the chord by drinking
or filling the wine
glasses until
a per
fect
U
N
I
S
O
N
is
fou
nd by all four
choruses of wine glasses.

Four groups of performers playing
wine glasses in four different ar
eas of a darkened, but candle
lit space gradually change
the chord by drinking
or filling the wine
glasses until
a per
fect
U
N
I
S
O
N
is
fou
nd by all four
choruses of wine glasses.

Four groups of performers playing
wine glasses in four different ar
eas of a darkened, but candle
lit space gradually change
the chord by drinking
or filling the wine
glasses until
a per
fect
U
N
I
S
O
N
is
fou
nd by all four
choruses of wine glasses.

KRISTALLNACHT, 1998
Four antiphonal choruses of
wine glasses.

On the night of 10 November 1938,
Nazi thugs in cities across
Germany smashed the windows
of Jewish shops and homes in
an act of racial violence known
as "Kristallnacht," the night of
broken glass. This work was
written on 10 November 1998
from the safety of another era,
as a meditation on the sixtieth
anniversary of the tragic event.

Montague seeks to alter the image
of a famous work by slowing it
down to its essence. The change,
like microscopic surgery, opens up
the piece to examine its various
elements in detail.

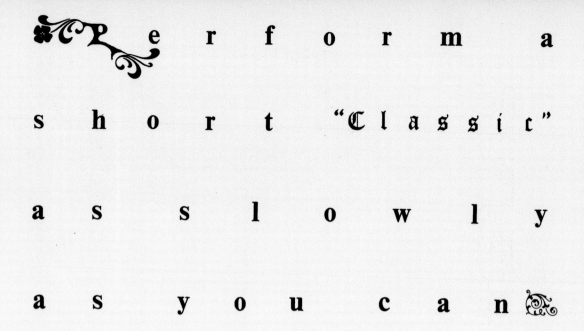

P e r f o r m   a

s h o r t   "Classic"

a s s   s l o w l y

a s   y o u   c a n

DUO, 1982
TRIO, 1976

Both works address the wide
variation of interpretation,
tempo and duration in different
performers' readings of the same
set of musical instructions,
i.e., the composer's score.
They also show the change when
the familiar musical elements—
harmony, rhythm, melody,
structure, form—are pushed
into kaleidoscopic distortion
by multiple, simultaneous
performances.

Record a famous "classic" in stereo

[— Start both tape and instrument(s), or voice(s) together —— at the same time. ———————]

* Perform your interpretation of the *work live* *

Record one interpretation of a famous work on CHANNEL 1

Record another interpretation of the same work on CHANNEL 2

Perform your own interpretation of the same work L I V E

[Start both tape and instrument (s), or voice (s) together — at the same time —]

Tigida Pipa

TIGIDA PIPA (page one), 1983–89

The text consists of invented words and percussive sounds. The rhythmic structure propels the performer through many sonic experiences. Inspired by some of Frank Denyer's text compositions, it was written for the London virtuoso vocal ensemble Singcircle.

THE SOUND OF TYPE

Established over a decade ago, Why Not Associates is a multidisciplinary design studio based in London. Their experimental attitude has been applied to such wide-ranging formats as postage stamps and large-scale exhibition design, from corporate identities to public art and film.

Of great importance to Why Not, is the client's willingness to share in the studio's spirit of adventure and invention. Why Not believes that people are much more receptive to adventurous design than is sometimes anticipated.

The visual soundbites in this section were created as dividers in an hour-long film that was shown at the Virgin Music Group conference. The sequences use typography and imagery to communicate visually the personalities of the various musicians featured.

JANET JACKSON
Based around Jackson's hatred of "girly flowery things," Why Not brutalized the flower image by inversing and distorting it in a series of frames that overlap one another.

LENNY KRAVITZ
Bold typography reflects the musician's heavy and calm voice. The type revolves around a centerpoint that gives the impression of a record spinning on a turntable.

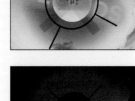

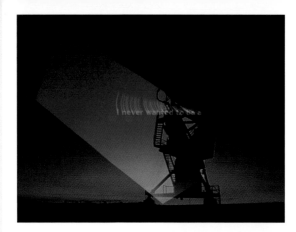

GEORGE MICHAEL
Letterforms sparkle and glitter like stars as they move in and out of a darkened skyscape. The sequence is consistent with the musician's image.

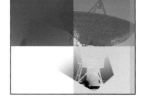

SMASHING PUMPKINS

The emphasis on the four-letter words "love," "duty" and "play" represents an optimistic simplicity verbalized by the band's introspective lead singer.

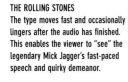

THE ROLLING STONES

The type moves fast and occasionally lingers after the audio has finished. This enables the viewer to "see" the legendary Mick Jagger's fast-paced speech and quirky demeanor.

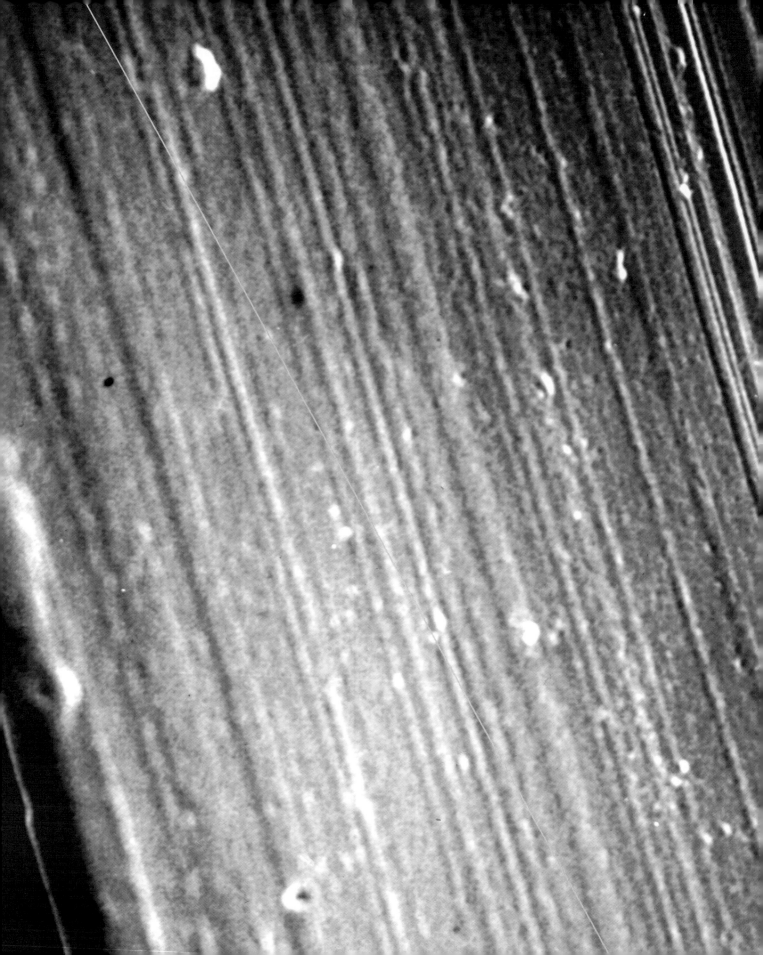

2

MATERIAL

Various methods of production, such as artistic and commercial, individual and collaborative, two-dimensional and three-dimensional, are employed by each studio. The resulting work shows technical and material proficiency; a signature or personal imprint of the artist or designer; and a meaning that transcends the original—in many cases commercial—function to become a self-contained, musically inspired artifact.

SEEING VOICES

Eikes Grafischer Hort, located in Frankfurt, Germany, constantly rotates its contributors to keep its design fresh. Since 1994, the "Hort's" (which means "hoard" or "treasure" in German) three-person team, which specializes in music-related design, has been assisted by performing artists, photographers, typographers and fine artists to meet clients' increasingly diverse needs. EGH has worked with such companies as Orbit Records, Virgin Records, BMG Music and Sony Music.

SUMMER EVENT
The poster promotes an open-air music and dance festival.

ORBIT RECORDS
An advertisement for Orbit Records thanks its DJs for their cooperation over 1999.

A1: MAURO PICOTTO REMIX 7.41 | B1: TOM WAX REMIX 8.16 | B2: TURN IN, TUNE OUT, DROP OUT (ORIGINAL MIX) 8.30

ALL TRACKS WRITTEN BY JENS ZIMMERMANN AND NOSIE KATZMANN. PRODUCED BY TORSTEN FENSLAU AND JENS ZIMMERMANN. DEVELOPMENT BY JENS ZIMMERMANN. BREATH OF LIFE BY NOSIE KATZMANN. ORIGINALLY CONSTRUCTED @ park000 STUDIOS, DARMSTADT. PUBLISHED BY ABFAHRT PUBLISHING / GET INTO MAGIC MUSIKVERLAG / WARNER CHAPPELL. TRACK A1 REMIXED BY MAURO PICOTTO. TRACK B1 REMIXED BY TOM WAX & THORSTEN ADLER @ PHUTURE WAX SOUNDLAB. "TURN IN, TUNE OUT, DROP OUT", MIXED BY TORSTEN FENSLAU & JENS ZIMMERMANN. SLEEVE DESIGNED BY RALF HIEMISCH & EIKE KÖNIG AT WWW.EIKESGRAFISCHERHORT.COM | SPECIAL THANKS TO TIM DOBROVOLNY. (P) + (C) 2000 ABFAHRT RECORDS GMBH. ABF 2001 | LC 5598 | DISTRIBUTED BY DISCOMANIA. MADE IN GERMANY. COME AND SEE US AT WWW.ABFAHRT-RECORDS.DE

ABFAHRT RECORDS GMBH, P.O. BOX: 11 01 63, 64216 DARMSTADT. TEL.: (+49) 06151/1768-0, FAX: (+49) 06151/226 14

TYRELL CORP.

On the release of the band's mini-album Running 2.0, EGH designed different covers for the CD, vinyl and remix vinyl. A continuity was established by the wire-frame figure that appears on all the covers, but is never seen in the same position or context.

DIVER + ACE
MENTAL THING

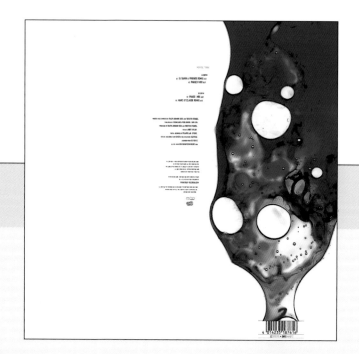

DIVER + ACE
Two sketches were produced for
this group's mini-album <u>Mental Thing</u>.
The first is derived from the
enlargement of patterns of colored
liquids. The second is based on
a series of illustrations developed
by Achim Reichert during his stay
in New York.

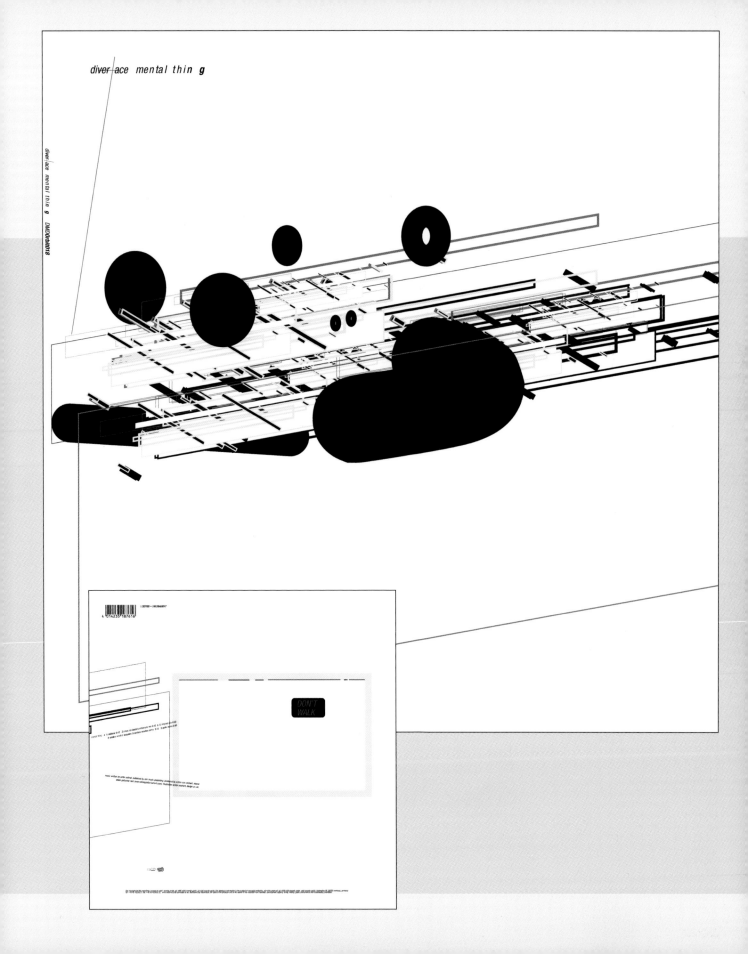

OLIVER LIEB
For the single "Subraumstimulation,"
EGH packed a record-player arm in ice.

CELVIN ROTANE
EGH created a living-room atmosphere
for the cover of <u>Houze Muzique</u>—
a kind of futuristic party set in the
comfort of one's home. On the back
cover [above], the studio reduced
the imagery to computer-generated,
auto-traced lines.

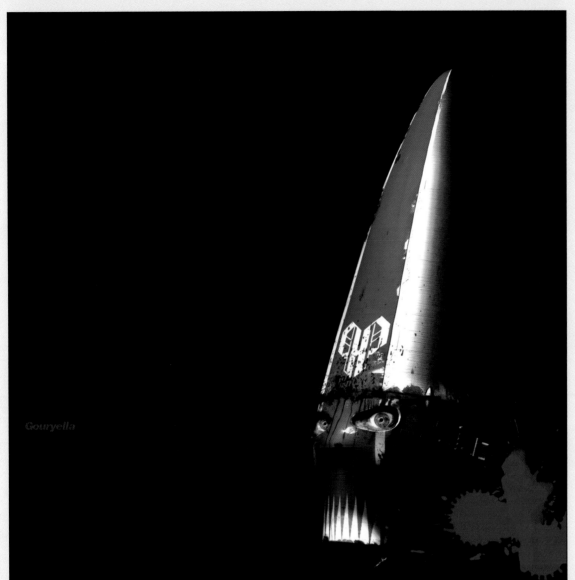

Gouryella

GOURYELLA
This illustration was originally designed for a "hardcore techno event," but the event promoter thought that it was too frightening, so EGH used it for the release of the single "Gouryella." The image was produced using 3-D software, except for the eyes, which were taken from photographs of real eyes to give a lifelike appearance.

FRIDGE
The studio created a collage-like angel (inspired by Aleksandr Rodchenko's exploration of photo collage) for the release of the band's mini-album. Zeppelins become wings, and a roll of adhesive tape forms a halo.

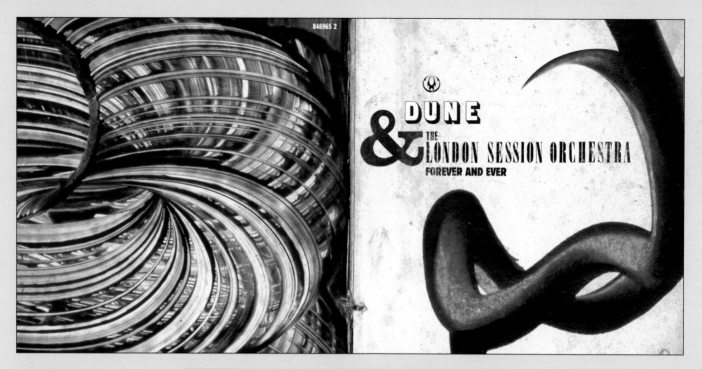

846965 2

DUNE
& THE LONDON SESSION ORCHESTRA
FOREVER AND EVER

DUNE & THE LONDON SESSION ORCHESTRA

Forever and Ever is the second compilation in a series of classical music cover versions. To continue the theme of the first publication, EGH used paper as the background and base material. The illustrations are actually the magnified scribbles of felt-tip pens, and it is astonishing how they become 3-D objects by the change of format. EGH combined these organic forms with metal objects, which had been abstracted from musical instruments.

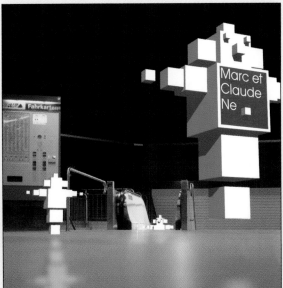

MARC ET CLAUDE
The title <u>A Tribute to Kraftwerk</u> indicates the purpose of the song. During the creation of these graphics, it was decided that the "block figures" would become the band's identity.

MARC ET CLAUDE
For the mini-album <u>NE</u>, EGH reproduced the block figures, which were created by using vector (line-based) graphics on 3-D software for better integration with the photographic spaces.

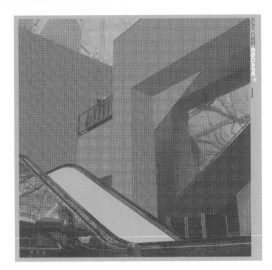

KAYCEE
KayCee's mini-album <u>Escape</u> is based around photographs taken at Frankfurt International Airport, i.e., flying as a means of escape. Escalators also feature as escape routes. On the back of each cover, this concept is further emphasized by a little boy [left], isolated in a large space.

The project involves painting over photographs, a medium in which designer Eike Koenig has much experience. Areas of the image are covered by monochromatic, solid fills. Other parts of the photograph show through and are untreated. The remix [above] uses the same materials, but is presented differently by monochromatic screening and coloring.

NORTHERN LIGHT

Founded in 1977 by Gert Dumbar, Studio Dumbar has become an integral part of Holland's visual landscape, from railway cars to restaurant signs. Prominent clients include Dutch Railways, Royal Dutch PTT, Dutch Automobile Association and the Dutch police. Studio Dumbar's influence can also be seen on the cultural scene, with such customers as North Sea Jazz Festival, Holland Dance Festival, Zeebelt Theatre and Amsterdam's Rijksmuseum.

NORTH SEA JAZZ FESTIVAL
Every year the organizers of this international festival invite several design studios to participate in what they term an "art-poster" competition.

For many years the festival has been situated near the beach in Scheveningen, In 1999, one of Studio Dumbar's designs combined location and music in a floating "Trumpetfish."

By letting it fly above the beach, the studio produced a strange, serene and surrealistic scene. The contrast between the computer-rendered metallic fish/instrument and the black-and-white 1930's letterforms showed the variety of musical styles at the festival.

This poster was inspired by the great jazz music that powerfully stirs up the city once a year. The organic shape represents the stormy weather and a trumpet.

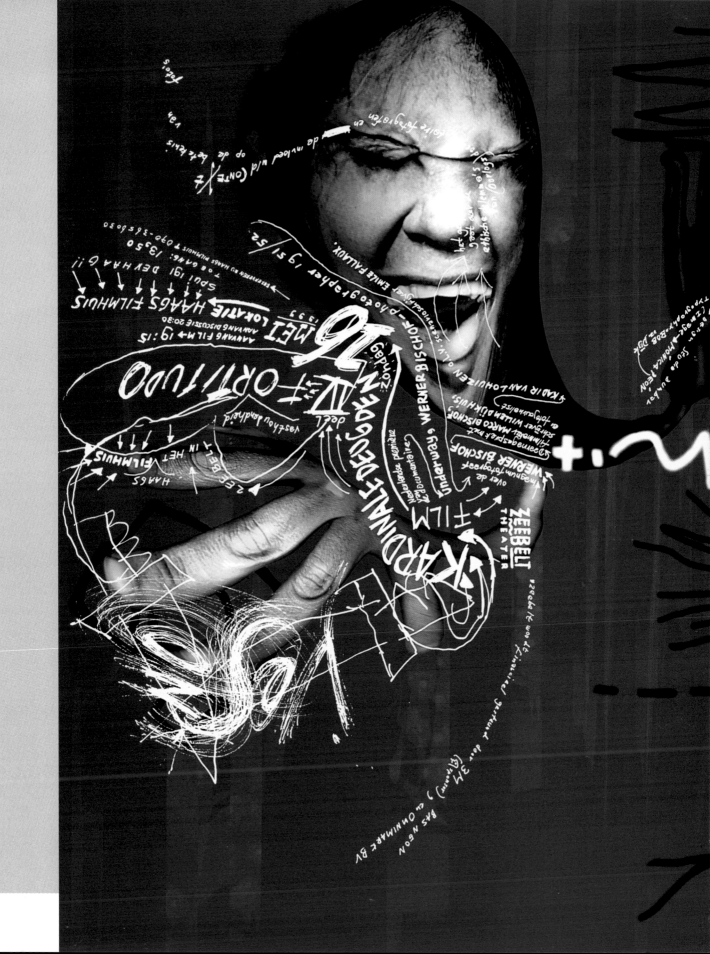

A number of performances at Zeebelt
Theatre focused on the Greek cardinal
virtues. In Plato's philosophy, these
virtues work together and culminate
in human perfection.

FORTITUDO [previous page]
An evening about fortitude and the
strength of mind that allows one to
endure pain or adversity with courage
is advertised on this poster.
A documentary was shown about
Magnum photographer Werner Bischof
and his internal struggle about the
ethics of his job. For example, is it
morbid to gain money through images
of human misery, or is it valid when
the images bring awareness of the
situation and, therefore, help?

JUSTITIA
The virtue of justice is explored in
this production: the principles of
truth, moral righteousness and
fair treatment.

PRUDENTIA
A performance was devoted to
prudence: the wisdom to make the
right choices, gained through
experience. Jaap Drupsteen, a leading
Dutch designer, tried to make Luciano
Berio's experimental music visually
accessible. He wanted the audience to
experience the music by looking with
their ears and hearing with their eyes.

An old, wise man is listening to music.
The organic shape connected to his
right ear suggests a visual translation
of the music. The text is written in the
shape of a piece of film and a
projector.

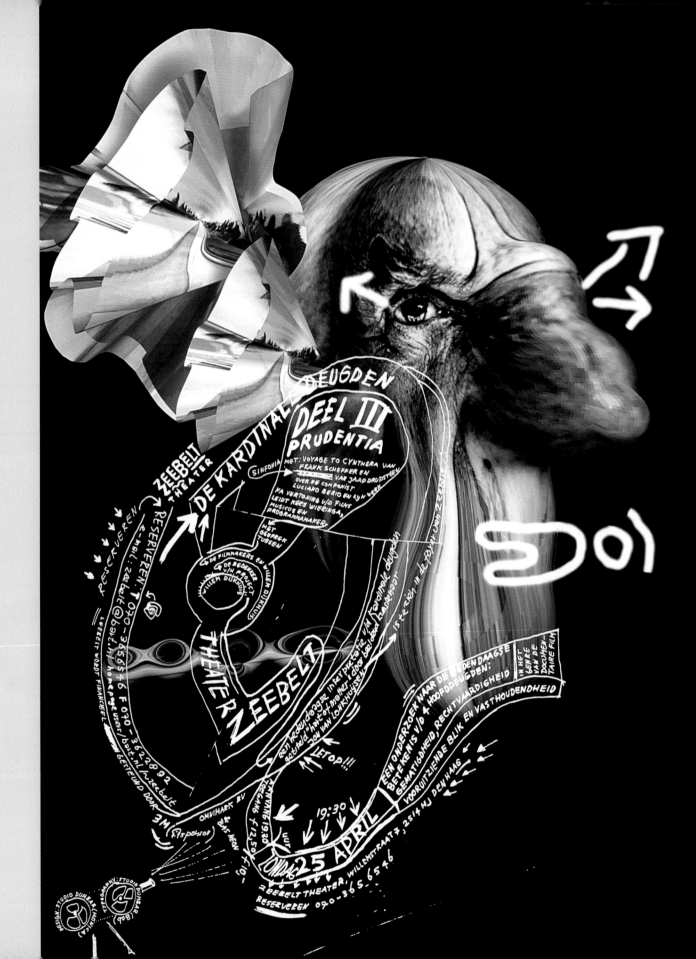

THE HOLLAND DANCE FESTIVAL
The theme chosen for the 1995 festival was "Music for Dance," resulting in posters where musical notes were combined with photographs of dancers. Notes not only represent music, they also look like a 2-D dance on paper and therefore connect music and movement.

Traditionally, musical notes are black, printed on a white background. So, by using black-and-white photographs in combination with the notes, a strong visual language was created. This poster series was easily recognizable and quite cheap to reproduce.

Designer Bob van Dijk suggested creating one poster for general information, three for the theaters where the festival took place and two for the main acts. This way, an interesting and lively event style was born.

THE HOLLAND DANCE FESTIVAL
In a dance festival, the choreographer and the resulting productions are normally the focal point. What made the 1998 festival different was that the director organized the program around the dancer and his or her individual qualities.

Emphasis in this poster series is on a personal approach. The choice of a black background means that the lighter image becomes isolated and more intimate. Individuality is portrayed by the use of parts of pictures to create completely new and unique "dancers" or "sculptures." The theme, "A Dancer's Tale," and the name of the festival were put on each poster in handwritten letterforms.

SONIC LANDSCAPES

3. incident at cima
6. carrying on to cadiz
9. chiriaco summit
predawn
ivanpah

kelso

Independent Project Press was born out of Bruce Licher's vision of combining music and packaging in a cohesive, artful and economical whole. Having spent almost a decade as a post-punk musician in Los Angeles, Licher's work with IPP and its sister record label, Independent Project Records, shows a startling change of pace for Licher and the design world at large. Using the almost extinct method of letterpress printing and such materials as chipboard and metallic ink, Licher conjures up the sense of the desert vernacular. Each piece is like a relic from a place far from the hustle and bustle of city life and from a time long before computers.

SCENIC
Bruce Licher, member of the band Scenic, has written soundtracks about the East Mojave Desert. The music captures the minimal and mysterious qualities of the desert landscape, but sound is only part of the experience. The patina of letterpress type, combined with Licher's grainy photographs, make the packaging an intrinsic element of the project. Both musically and visually, the result is an engaging marriage of form and technique.

scenic

Bruce Licher GUITARS **Brock Wirtz** DRUMS **James Brenner** BASS

HAND LETTERPRESS PRINTED BY
WILLIAM FAIRCLOTH & BRUCE LICHER

INDEPENDENT PROJECT RECORDS

Post Box 1033 §§§ Sedona §§§ Arizona 86339

Nº 3419

First Edition - 3500 copies
FEBRUARY 1995

THE INCIDENT AT CIMA
The album cover, printed on gypsum
board, is a deft balance of panoramas
and white space.

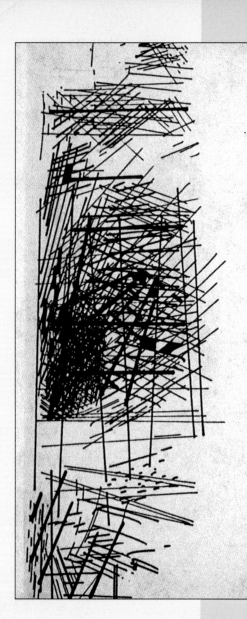

TONE
the guitar ensemble

BUILD

TONE
Members of this guitar ensemble refer to their music as "math-rock." For the cover of their album Build, Licher used geometric line drawings and sparse typography to successfully evoke the band's sound.

TONE
the guitar ensemble

JOSH BENNETT
guitar
TOM BERARD
2nd bass
JUSTIN CHEARNO
guitar 1,3,4
GEORDIE GRINDLE
guitar 1,3,4
GREGG HUDSON
percussion
KEVIN KIM
guitar
MICHAEL MILLS
guitar 2,5,6
MITCH PARKER
guitar
ADAM RUTLAND
guitar 2,5,6
NORM VEENSTRA
lead bass 4,5,6; monotone guitar 1,2; vibrato guitar 3
JIM WILLIAMSON
guitar 1,3,4

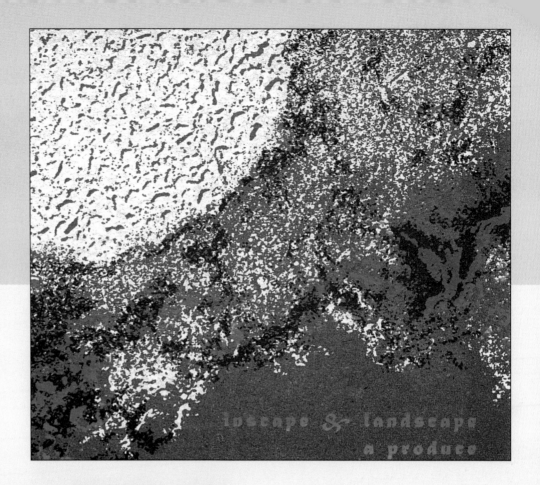

A PRODUCE
The cover of the group's CD
<u>Inscape & Landscape</u> was
designed by Licher's wife, Maria.
She manipulated a photograph
of the earth and then made
photoengraving plates for the
letterpress. There are two cover
variations, "hot" and "cool"; one is
reddish-brown and the other gray.

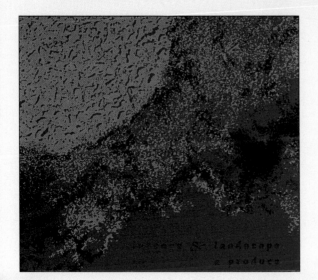

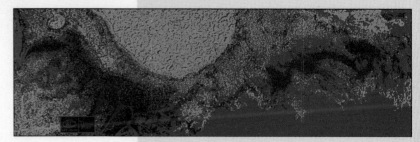

TONE
the guitar ensemble
BUILD

SCENIC

In the middle of the remote Eastern Mojave Desert stands the Kelso Depot. Built in 1924 in the then popular style of the early Spanish missions, it supplied meals and overnight accommodations for train crews on the long haul across the desert from Los Angeles. Located about 300 miles from Las Vegas, the town of Kelso was a much-needed oasis in the era of steam locomotives, and the Depot served the small desert community for over sixty years before being closed in 1985. In the years since, the building has fallen into disrepair, however through the efforts of various groups the Kelso Depot is in the process of being restored. Plans are for it to become a visitors center for the East Mojave National Scenic Area, where travellers can learn about the history of this unique and special area. For further information regarding the restoration, write to the Kelso Depot Fund at P.O. Box 1346, Barstow, CA 92312.

scenic / lanterna
live recordings
parasol records PAR-031 / independent project records IP 058
33 1/3
r.p.m.

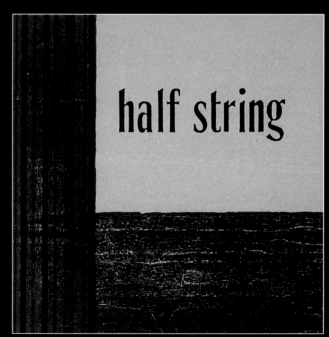

half string

THE VERNACULAR
The consistent visual language of
Independent Project Records seems
to rise from the landscape and play
music for the eyes.

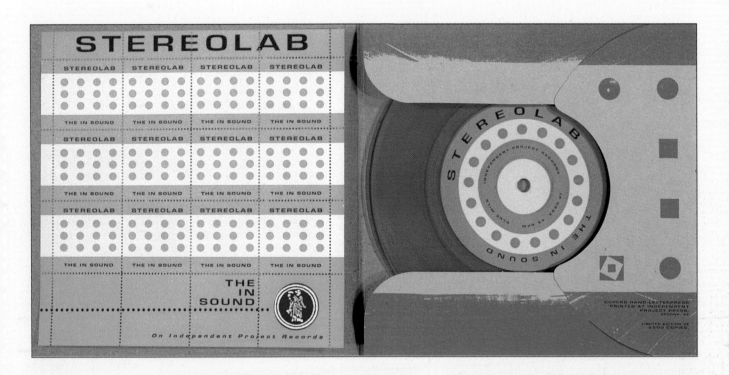

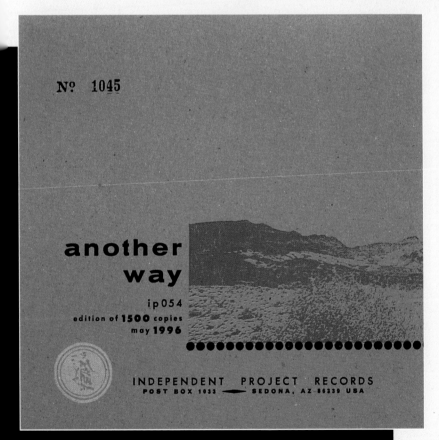

STEREOLAB
This European avant-rock quintet's very modern sound and IPP's antiquated style would at first seem to make an uncomfortable partnership. For the album The In Sound, however, Licher played on the awkwardness of the pairing to create a sleeve that is at once evocative of Stereolab's space-age sound, but also true to IPP's weathered aesthetic.

ITALIAN RENAISSANCE

Fabio Berruti has worked in the diverse fields of photography, fashion design, advertising, packaging design and publishing, and is now established as a successful graphic designer. Infinite Studio, located in Berruti's native Italian village of Albisola Superior, has made its presence felt in the music industry in both the Italian and French markets, claiming such high-profile clients as BMG Music, Warner Music, Sony Music and EMI Music. Berruti frequently combines several of his skills in one project; for example, he used photographs from his own portfolio for the Italian violinist Uto Ughi's CD covers [see opposite]. For Italian singer and composer Daniele Silvestri's album [below], Berruti was also responsible for the packaging design.

FERRUCCIO BUSONI, pianist
CD covers

DANIELE SILVESTRI, singer/composer
Sig. Dapatas CD cover

VACA ROSSI, rock singer
CD-single cover

UTO UGHI, violinist
CD covers

THE FACE
OF MUSIC

Publisher, type foundry and record label, Emigre tries to unite the music it releases with its interest in graphic design. As the digital production of music and design becomes more and more frequent, reducing musical notes and visual marks to a mathematical sequence and combining them on compact disk seems logical.

The firm represents independent musicians who have the ability and courage to experiment, surpassing the restrictive and formulaic environment of popular music. Emigre advocates music that, because of its noncommercial nature, would not otherwise have been released.

Emigre focuses on small print-runs, limited editions and other rare and experimental projects, both verbal and visual, including but not limited to exhibition catalogs, multimedia CDs, essays and magazines.

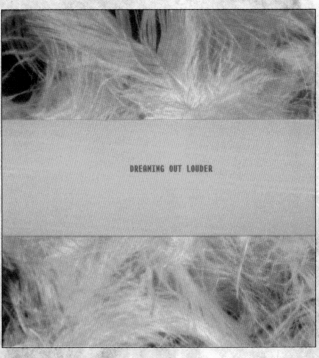

ITCHY PET

This is second in a series of three music releases that, "may or may not be related," according to designer Rudy VanderLans. It is a compilation of digital sampling infused with verse, repetitious percussion and throbbing bass. The project was produced, performed, arranged and recorded on computer by multi-instrumentalist Erik Deerly.

The limited-edition packaging uses hyper-magnified printer dot patterns to form images of farm animals. The sixteen-page full-color booklet was designed and printed as a poster, which was then folded, bound and trimmed. Feathers that at once relate to the name of the project and reflect the nature of the recorded sounds are also included in a custom-made box.

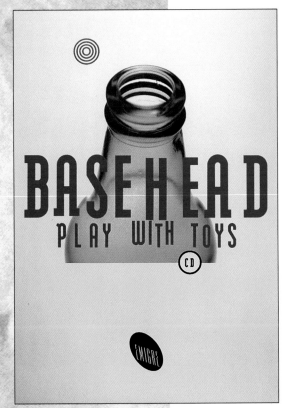

POSTERS
A series of promotional posters announced music releases to the press, stores and distributors.

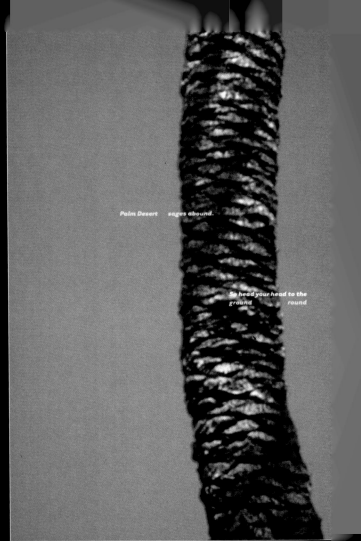

Palm Desert *sages abound.*

So head your head to the ground *round*

Left unsung as I have strung the frame

on the banks of vanity

PALM DESERT
This is the first book of photographs by the creator of <u>Emigre Magazine</u> Rudy VanderLans. It is based on the music and lyrics of Los Angeles–based composer Van Dyke Parks. Somewhere between fact and fantasy, the book visualizes the environment evoked in Parks's 1968 composition "Palm Desert." It also echoes his creative approach by blending classical, historical, vernacular and environmental themes. The result is a dynamic combination of a fan's tribute, documentary photography, impressionism, and an experimental music review.

JUST THE GOOD OL' BOYS

Hatchshow Print, a 120-year-old letterpress facility in Nashville, Tennessee, creates posters for members of the country music industry. The six-person firm handles all aspects of production, from design to printing and they have a vast archive of original artwork. In addition to posters, Hatchshow Print produces book and CD covers. Presented on these pages is a selection from the company's rich visual history.

PICK IT UP
BILL MONROE
LIVE FROM MOUNTAIN STAGE
BLUE PLATE MUSIC

MOUNTAIN STAGE is produced by West Virginia Public Radio & can be heard nation wide on Public Radio International. BPM-400
www.OHBOY.com   HATCH SHOW PRINT · NASHVILLE, TN · m.fred   1.800.521.2112

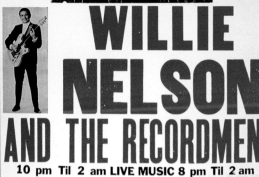

BONANZA CLUB
8 MILES ON HIGHWAY 62 WEST

OPEN 12 NOON DAILY   Phone 353-9746

THUR. NOV. 5
IN PERSON
WILLIE NELSON
AND THE RECORDMEN
10 pm Til 2 am LIVE MUSIC 8 pm Til 2 am

NASHVILLE MUNICIPAL AUD. NOV. 16 & 17

Shows Sat. 2 & 8 P.M. Sun. 1:30 & 5 P.M.

NASHVILLE POLICE BENEFIT ASSOCIATION
IN COOPERATION WITH
MARTHA WHITE MILLS

PRESENT
IN PERSON
AMERICA'S FAVORITE

BEVERLY HILLBILLIES

GRANNY - JETHRO
and ELLY MAY

PLUS MANY GREAT CIRCUS ACTS

AND

| The WILBURN BROS. with DON HELMS & LORETTA LYNN (SATURDAY SHOWS ONLY) | Lester FLATT & Earl SCRUGGS & the Foggy Mountain Boys (SUNDAY SHOWS ONLY) |

Admission Advance $2.00   at Door $2.50   Children Under 12 $1.00

Tickets Available at Aud. or any Policeman

Children Under 12 Admitted FREE with Martha White Flour or Meal Label 5 - lb. or Larger

C ☆ 1996 Hatch Show Print

Printed from the original plates.

COUNTY FAIR AUD.
BLOOMFIELD HIWAY - FARMINGTON, N. M.
2 PERFORMANCES 4:00 & 8:00 P. M
SUN. JULY 30

ADV. TICKETS ON SALE AT CUSTOM HI FI - TV SPECIALIST, KWYK - KRZE
ADV. $1.50, AT DOOR $2.00, CHILDREN $1.00 (At All Times Under 12)

GRAND OLE OPRY

"SPEND AN EVENING WITH MARTY ROBBINS"
● IN PERSON ●

MARTY ROBBINS
AND THE
TEAR DROPS BAND

HATCH SHOW PRINT, Nashville, Tenn.   Printed from the original plates.

DESTRUCTIVE ORDER

In the conservative German-speaking Swiss capital of Bern, the cutting-edge design of BüroDestruct seems out of place. In fact, the very name of the studio (founded in 1992) is contradictory. A "Büro" is a place of orderly and careful behavior, while "Destruct" suggests devastation and change. BüroDestruct's work features tortured, distorted imagery, three-dimensionality and aggressive typography, all of which have been reduced and refined to fit the traditional pattern of Swiss graphic design since Josef Müller-Brockmann. The firm maintains fresh visual language by keeping its hands, eyes and ears on the music and club scene and by exchanging research results with the Japanese firm Cyclone Graphix.

The following pages present flyers and posters for drum'n'bass clubnights and concerts.

big berner beats

from schlepp-hop
to fett-breakz ブレイク.クビーーツ

FRI
20.03.98 taifun/clubraum
in order of appearance: ROTE FABRIK ZÜRICH
23:00
LODEL FIZLER, BOBA FETT, DIFERENZ, SPECTRON
büro destruct   wasserwerk   xtra records   mokka/drs3

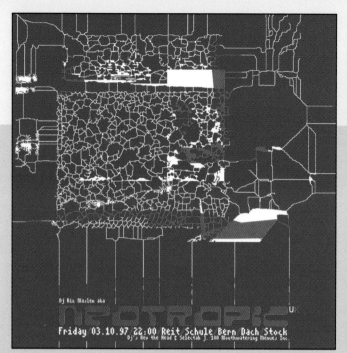

Dj Riz Maslen aka

NEOTROPIC

Friday 03.10.97 22:00 Reit Schule Bern Dach Stock
Dj's Rev the Head & Selectah J. 100 Mouthwatering Menues Inc.

SCHALTKREIS #00002

FRI. 12-02-99 GASKESSEL SANDRAINSTR 25
3007 BERN 0313724900
22:00-03:30 AFTERHOUR-INFO AT NIGHT

DJ DEE TREE 9
DJ PRINCESS P
DJ PULP

IN KONZERT: FUTURE LOOP FOUNDATION (UK)

OFFENE TURE: 22:00

VORVERKAUF: RECORD JUNKIE, KRAMGASSE 8, BERN

UK

**FUTURE: LOOP
FOUNDATION**
DJ MICHEAL DOG (PLANET DOG, UK)
FREITAG 30. JANUAR 1998
REITSCHULE DACHSTOCK BERN

Holy Moments
büro discotec

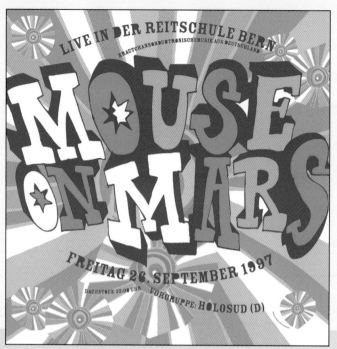

LIVE IN DER REITSCHULE BERN
KRAUTCHANSONSUBURTRONISCHEMUSIK AUS DEUTSCHLAND

MOUSE ON MARS

FREITAG 26. SEPTEMBER 1997

DACHSTOCK 22:00 UHR   VORGRUPPE: HOLOSUD (D)

CLEAR

ELECTRONIC DEPT. PRESENTS   CLEAR RECORDS LABELNIGHTER
BERN REITSCHULE-DACHSTOCK-FRIDAY 21 NOV. 97 DOORS 22:00
FEAT LIVE REFLECTION(JAPAN) MORGAN GEIST(USA), METAMATICS(UK)
DJ´S KIRK DE GIORGIO,DEEPHEART, CLAIR AND HAL
SPECIAL GUEST DJ´S HIDDEN AGENDA(METALHEADZ) AND 4HERO(REINFORCED)
VORVERKAUF RECORD JUNKIE KRAMGASSE 8 BERN
DFS LOPETZYT WWW.BERMODA.CH/BUREAUDESTRUCT

David Holmes Belfast, Northern Ireland
appearing as dj
support dj Curly
Reitschule Bern Dachstock
Vorverkauf: Record Junkie, Kramgasse 8, Bern
Don't design just yet Lopetz98:büro destruct

FR 10 04 98 21:30

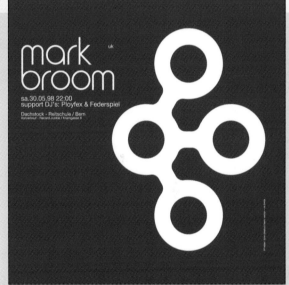

mark uk
broom
sa.30.05.98 22:00
support DJ's: Ployfex & Federspiel
Dachstock - Reitschule / Bern
Vorverkauf : Record Junkie / Kramgasse 8

dj's
SAT:22.AUGUST.98 22:00
PROTOTYPE/METALHEADZ/NO-U-TURN UK
ED RUSH/TRACE
DJ   SENSI, UTR/BE
DRUM'N'BASS
REITSCHULE BERN DACHSTOCK
VORVERKAUF: RECORD JUNKIE, KRAMGASSE 8, BERN
LOP ETZ98:BÜRO DESTRUCT MC

METALHEADZ/VALVE UK
LEMON D/DILLINJA
/GUEST MC.................
GEORGE GEE (UNITED TRIBES)   VORVERKAUF: RECORD JUNKIE, KRAMGASSE 8, BE
DRUM'N'BASS   DATE   SAT:03.APR.99 22:00
REITSCHULE DACHSTOCK BERN

PESHAY
METALHEADZ/MOWAX UK
DJ SOULSOURCE

REITSCHULE
DACHSTOCK BERN
DRUM'N'BASS

VORVERKAUF: RECORD JUNKIE, KRAMGASSE 8, BE

dj's

FR'02'07'99
DATE   22:00

BÜRO DISCOTEC

FREITAG 21. JANUAR 2000/22.30
FOYER INTERNATIONAL
KULTURHALLEN DAMPFZENTRALE BERN
<DJ LODEL FIZLER & HGB FIDELJUS (BD BE)/RAINBOW (BE)
SELECTAH-J/KEV THE HEAD (100°MM. BE)/TEKJAM (2H)
VIDEOBEAMS.TOKYO-<CITY/J-POP-CHARTS
BÜRO DISCOTEC 7"INCH RELEASE
WWW.BERMUDA.CH/BD/DISCOTEC.HTML

produced in berlin
toni thiel & max losterbauer   www.bbtt.com   kitchen   sun sector
thomas fehlmann   www.bbtt.com/sunelectric/   asak!   lopat@bermuda.ch
                                                                        30.7.94   www.bermuda.ch/buerosudestruct
                                                                        present

SUN
ELECTRIC"
&DJ THOMAS FEHLMANN FROM THE ORB SOUND SYSTEM
THURSDAY 23.OCTOBRE.1997
REITSCHULE BERN DACHSTOCK
21:00

DRUM'N'BASS

Randall+Storm
RANDALL+STORM

RANDALL UK
METALHEADZ
DJ SOULSOURCE

VORVERKAUF: RECORD JUNKIE, KRAMGASSE 8, BERN

22:00

REITSCHULE
DACHSTOCK BERN
DATE FR'07'04'00

VISUAL IMPROVISATION

P2, a design studio based in New York City, has assembled a portfolio of commercial and personal work stemming from a wide range of audiovisual media (print, digital, film, video). Some of the most dynamic work comes from the designers' own experimentation, which runs fast and free from the constraints dictated by clients and commerce.

ONLINE MUSIC NETWORK PROMOTION
These poster studies are for a website that promotes an exchange of resources between the music industry, independent musicians and music fans. P2 developed two approaches to the promotion campaign, which included a poster, postcard, banners, press kit and stationery. One treatment [left] incorporates symbols that are found on music production and playback equipment. The other scheme [above] uses photographs of the LED indicator to emphasize texture and form.

POLYPROPYLENE STUDIES
P2 developed a logo and a series of images around the sonic textures of the experimental music collective Polypropylene. The designers attempted to translate visually a measure of music into a graphic environment of photographic appearance and gestural lines.

DWELLING

Presented here is the cover for a New York City—based alternative music group's debut album <u>My Brother the Cloud</u>. P2 was given a focusing target (which assists in the aiming of an artillery device) used by one of the band member's grandfathers in World War II, and was asked to incorporate it into the design of the CD packaging. The studio created a logo and graphic language around the symbol.

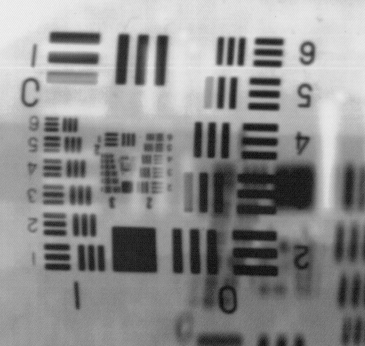

DWELLING

DWELLING

BACK COVER   FRONT COVER

DWELLING

1.

KEREN DEBERG
P2 created a graphic landscape around
original photography of Deberg's
career in pop music. The studio
also developed a subtext of graphic
icons as a narrative backdrop for
her EP/CD packaging.

inside

SLIDE SHOW AND CONCERT

The lyrical narratives of Rosey, a musician based in New York, were interpreted by P2 to produce a series of 116 slides. The eight songs had the added visual dimension of projected images that transformed the space by showing different locations, themes and abstractions. Each song had a unique group of images that flickered in rhythm to the tune and that were punctuated by the song titles.

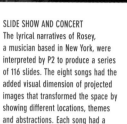

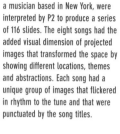

PARK
OPEN 24 HRS

CAR WASH
TAXI $2 95 OPEN 24 HOURS

Perfect

Afterlife

CULTURE IN CONCERT

How does a presenter of art present itself? Brooklyn Academy of Music's (BAM) design mission is to seduce visually an audience into participating in risky, mind-opening experiences with art and artists. In 1995, Michael Beirut's design team at Pentagram created a powerful visual identity [background image and below], intended to lure more New Yorkers across the bridge to the academy, one of the country's leading venues of contemporary performing arts. Ever since, this identity has been nurtured and transformed by the internal design department at BAM to create an integrated family of visual marketing materials that grows with the institution. Their strategy for the 1999–2000 season was to form an emotional appeal to an e-generation that is more diverse, well-traveled and jaded than the "boomers" who traditionally came to BAM. They use the chaotic energy of drum and bass, static electricity and rave culture to position BAM as the sexiest art experience in town.

Hiyomeki

Sankai Juku

BAMcafé
The visual identity for BAMcafé
is metaphoric; the letters on the cup
interact with the table top in much
the same way as artists interact with
the stage. The cup is placed by a
waiter on the table, shifted to the
left to make room for a plate, then
moved to the right to allow for
another diner. It's lifted for a re-fill
and brought to the mouth. In this
manner, the cup serves as an actor
on the stage (the table) in a production
(the dining experience).

PLAYING THE CONCEPTS

Stefan Sagmeister opened his firm less than ten years ago, but has already established himself as an important force in shaping CD packaging for a wide variety of clients in the music industry. "We opened with a plan to be a design house for music," Sagmeister recalls, and his approach to each project goes beyond simply conceiving a series of standard visuals. Before designing the packaging, Sagmeister likes to become familiar with the musicians' personalities, the instruments, the lyrics and the specific theme of the CD. This ensures that the design is an innovative synthesis of printing and packaging methods, image and materials that catch the attention of the eyes, ears and hands.

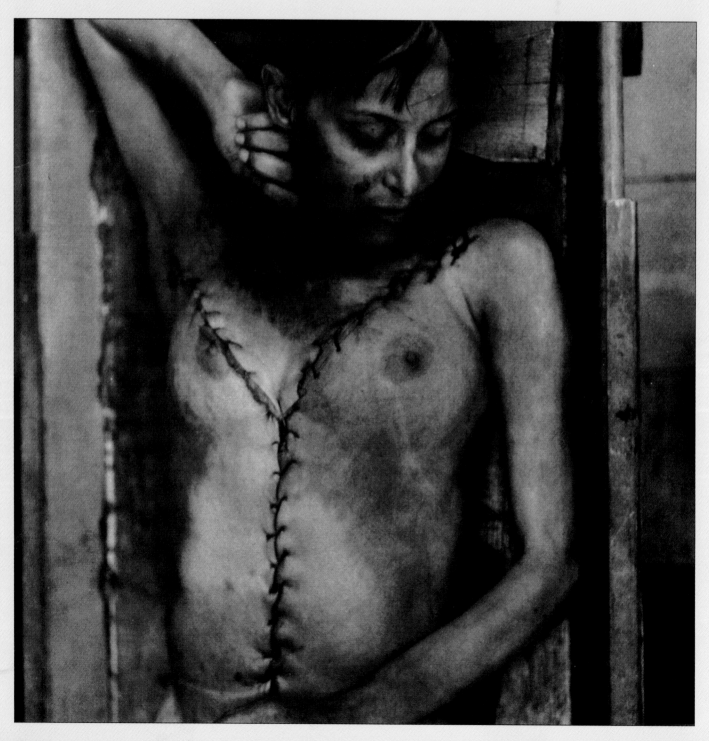

PRO-PAIN
On the first or second listening to the album <u>The Truth Hurts</u>, the music attacks the eardrums like coarse sandpaper. However, on the third play the music reveals an underlying beauty.

The same could be said of the morgue photographs that appear on the front of the CD. The woman died in her sleep and her body was opened to determine the cause of death. No retouching was done. All the pictures in the CD booklet are from the police records in the Municipal Archives of New York.

PRO-PAIN
THE TRUTH HURTS

The CD <u>Telling Stories</u> is a compilation of music, with Portuguese influence, from the African islands of Cape Verde and São Tomé. The packaging design unifies the wide range of lyrics and artists. Sagmeister die-cut a hole through the entire CD booklet and placed an image of the moon on the cover to express the Taoist notion of "nothingness."

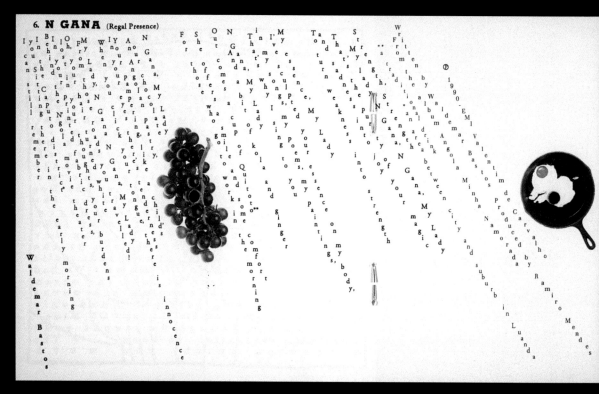

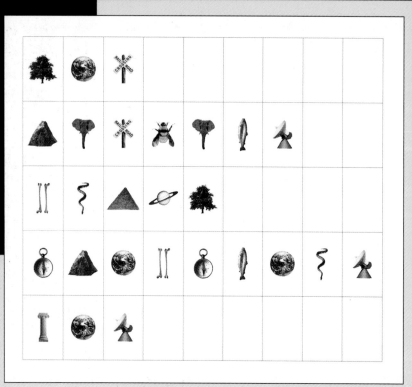

PAT METHENY GROUP
Sagmeister replaced all the type on the cover of the CD <u>Imaginary Day</u> with code. The images connect to the songs and mood of the album, and can be decoded by using the diagram printed on the disk itself.

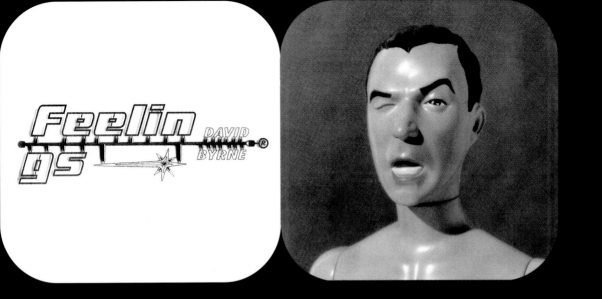

DAVID BYRNE, 1997
Round-cornered packaging for the CD
<u>Feelings</u> features dolls of the musician
in various emotional states: happy,
angry, sad, content. The design includes
a sophisticated, color-coded "David
Byrne mood computer," printed on
and under the actual disk, which
lets the listener determine his or
her current feelings while experiencing
the music. The letterforms were
constructed as models and were
then photographed.

H.P. ZINKER

When Stefan Sagmeister first arrived in New York, he saw an old and distinguished man approaching him on the sidewalk. As he passed Sagmeister, the man started shouting obscenities at no one in particular.

The lyrics of the album <u>Mountains of Madness</u> address schizophrenia and the different ways in which the city can make you "sick in the head."

The old man reappeared in the mind of the designer and he asked Tom Schierlitz to photograph an old man in calm and frantic states, the first printed in green and the second overprinted in red. When the booklet is slipped into the red-tinted CD case, the green image turns black and the red image becomes invisible.

SKELETON KEY

With reference to the CD's title <u>Fantastic Spikes Through Balloon</u>, Sagmeister photographed all balloonlike objects he could think of, for example, a sausage, a fart cushion and a blowfish. A matrix of holes was punched through the booklet to emphasize the theme and to create a unique texture.

The band did not want their audience to read the lyrics while listening to the music, so Sagmeister printed the words in reverse and they can only be read when reflected in the disk's mirror surface.

EYE SOUNDS

French designer Philippe Savoir studied at Duperré, the Parisian school of applied arts, and went on to work for six years in television, movies, advertising and animation. He creates CD covers, logos and theater posters and has produced all the design material for France's Orchestre National de Jazz since 1995. He has also worked with such music labels as Universal, Sony and Warner.

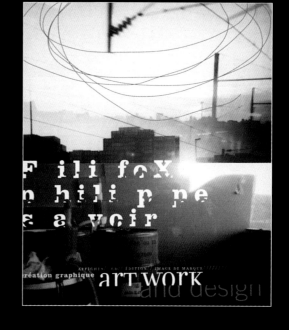

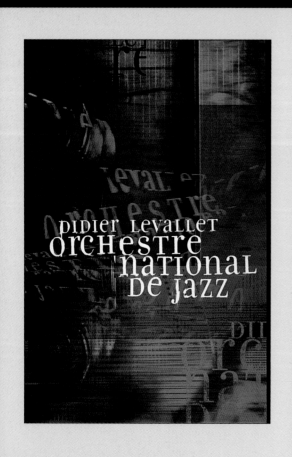

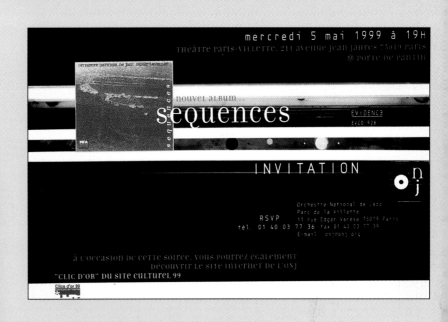

ORCHESTRE NATIONAL DE JAZZ
Savoir's research focuses on the relationship between text and image and the fusion of the two, resulting in the inevitable creation of multiple levels of reading. As a designer, Savoir is less interested in a particular style or product than he is in understanding the world of sights and sounds around him. Shown here is promotional material for the orchestra's concerts.

ORCHESTRE NATIONAL DE JAZZ
On the CD covers for <u>Reminiscing</u>
and <u>In Tempo</u>, Savoir captures the
complexity and intensity of
improvisational jazz. He uses
intricately layered color photographs
of details of instruments, combined
with graphic interpretations of
instruments and sound.

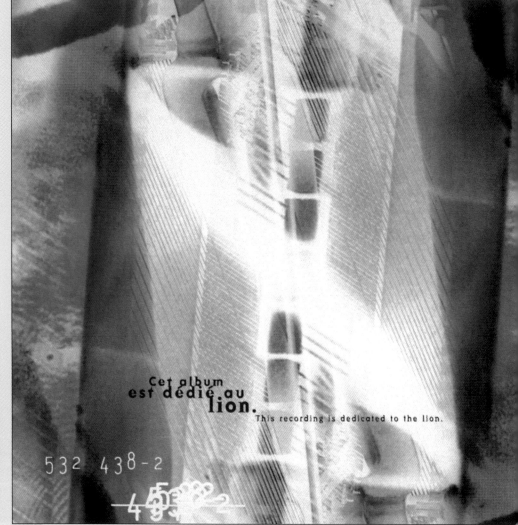

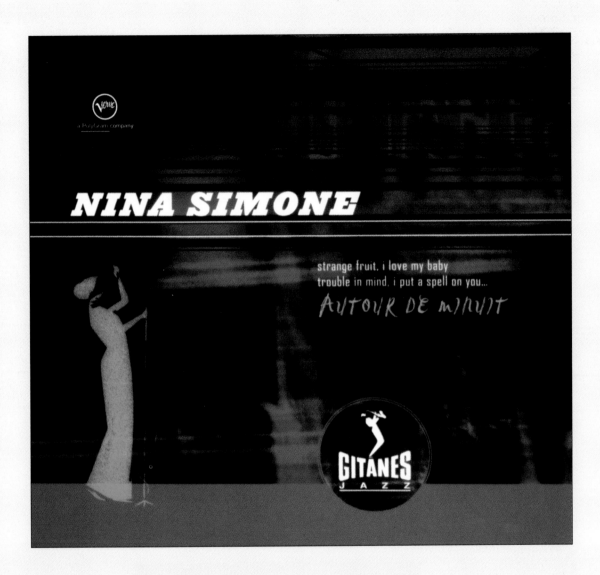

GITANES JAZZ

Representing only a sample of a fifty-one-volume jazz and blues CD series, these covers bring together the diverse styles and periods within these musical genres. Savoir developed a series style, but used color coding and simple, ghostlike silhouettes of each performer to make each cover unique. The emotions, mystery and nostalgia of this collection of legendary musicians are cleverly portrayed by Savoir's visual language. Frozen in time, the covers almost allow one to hear the music before the disk is played.

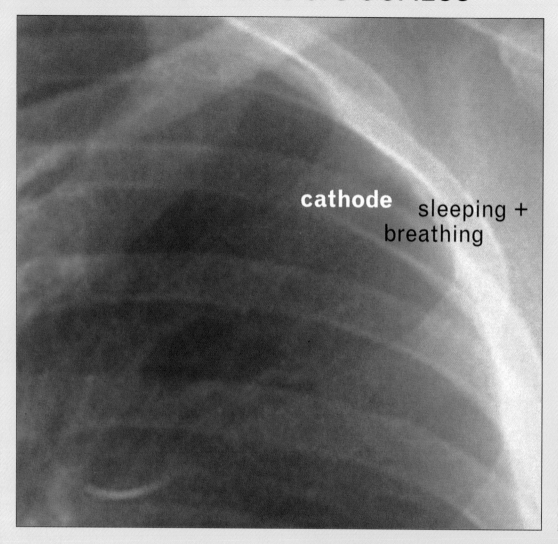

cathode

sleeping +
breathing

CATHODE
The band composes minimal
instrumental music with guitar,
bass, drums and the occasional
background keyboard. These images
were chosen for their simplicity and
because they reflect the name
of the band and the CD title
sleeping + breathing.

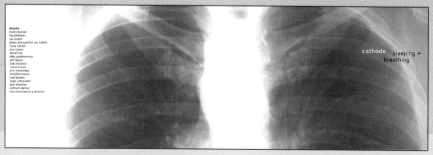

cathode   sleeping +
           breathing

Clifford Stoltze has been practicing design in Boston since obtaining his BFA from the University of Massachusetts in 1978. He established his multidimensional studio Stoltze Design in 1984, and it has since grown in size and received many prestigious awards. Stoltze's extensive project list includes corporate identities, publications, packaging, environmental and website design. Although not confined to a particular style, the studio is known for its sophisticated, unconventional design solutions and its passion for typography.

Stoltze is equally passionate about music. A former musician, he felt frustrated by the lack of music-related design, and five years ago became a partner in the Boston-based independent record label Castle von Buhler. Providing all the design services for the label gives Stoltze the freedom to experiment and have fun. Current music projects include a three-CD compilation with the record label Ellipsis Arts.

HAYHOUSE
The design of a twelve-CD collection gave much emphasis to the packaging materials to create individuality.

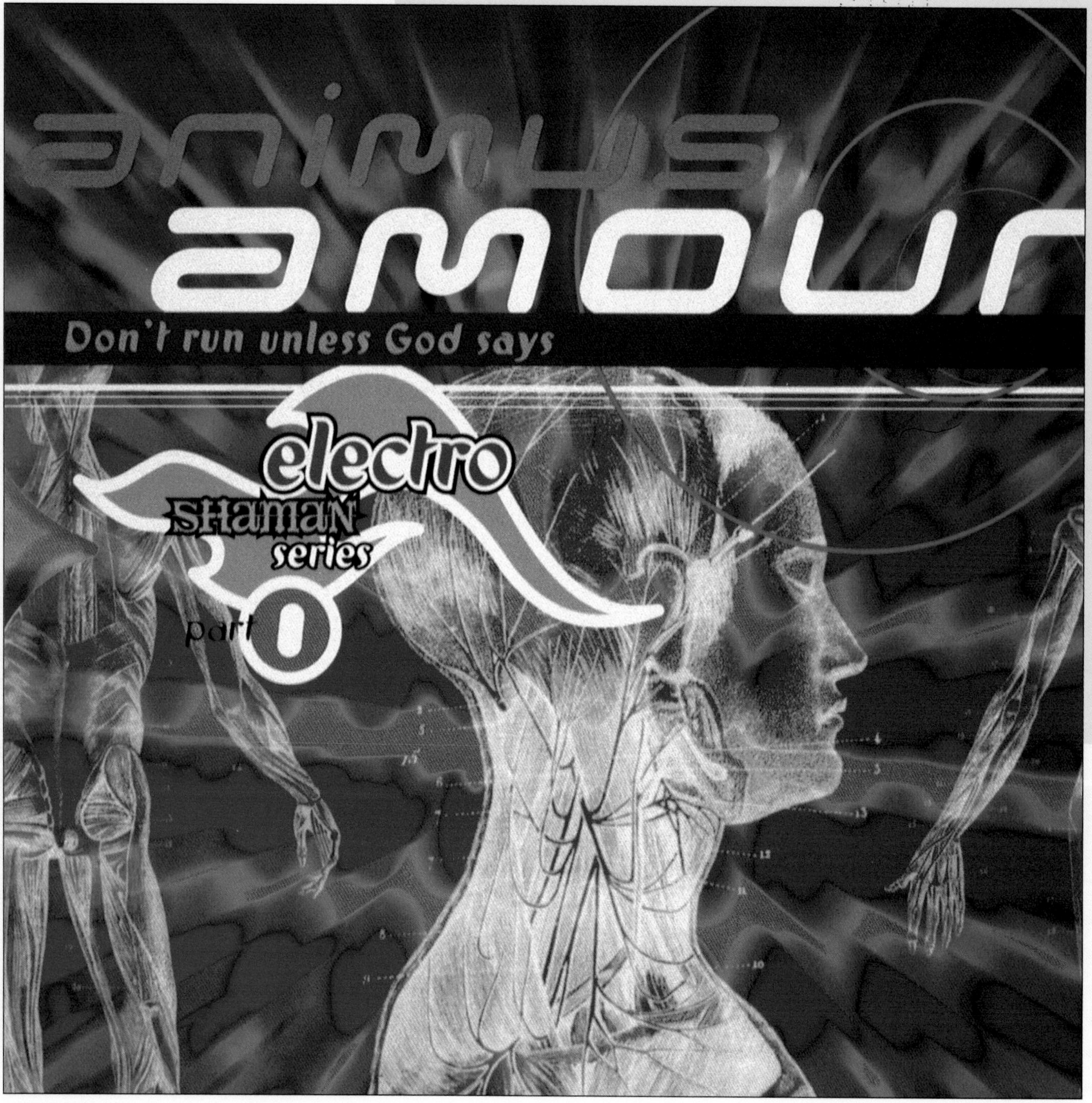

animus shmine
amour
Don't run unless God says

electro
SHAMAN
series
part 1

Don't Run Unless God Says

animus amour
richard west (aka Mr. C)
jeremy jones

Visit the Animus Amour Website: www.animusamour.com

For information or a catalog:
Ellipsis Arts...
P.O. Box 305
Roslyn, N.Y. 11576
Phone: (800) 788-6670
Fax: (516) 621-2750
www.ellipsisarts.com

℗© 1999 Ellipsis Arts
All rights reserved

Text written by
Mr. C and Jeremy Jones

Project Coordinator
Russell Charno D.C.

A & R
Wendy Motchan

Editor
Jim Tremayne

Design
Stoltze Design, Boston

No part of this book may be used or reproduced in any manner whatsoever without permission except in the case of brief quotations embodied in critical articles and reviews.

ANIMUS AMOUR
This is the first CD in the Electro Shaman series (a platform for artists exploring the terrain of expanded consciousness through electronic dance music) put out by Ellipsis Arts. Anatomical illustrations were superimposed over trippy computer-enhanced patterns, inspired by the photographs of sound mixing boards (devices that sample and mix sounds when recording music) supplied by the artist.

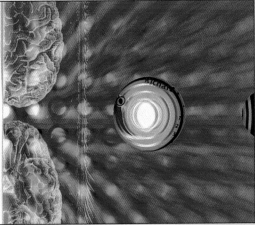

MUSIC BY:
SYMBION PROJECT
TURKISH DELIGHT
ORBIT
SPLASHDOWN
VERONICA BLACK MORPHEOUS NIPPLE
PELL MELL
COPPÉ
MARGO VS. THUNDERBALL
WOMEN OF SODOM
THE MOORS
EARDRUM U.K.
THE CURTAIN SOCIETY
MAX
SURAN SONG IN STAG
GREEN AND YELLOW T.V.
THE ROBBER WHO ROBBED THE TOWN
FELIDAE CHANT
MILE WIDE
VASTLESSSMUDGE
BETWIXT
CATHODE

~nigh~

NIGH
Third in a series of art/music compilations, this multifaceted project was used to promote illustrators and musicians and to raise money for AIDS. The challenge was to economically produce a custom-made CD package that would hold twenty-three postcards. Each song was interpreted by a different illustrator. The cover art is by William Tisdale, who died of AIDS in 1996.

SYMBION PROJECT [top]
This illustration was designed by David Miller for the band's song "Tcejorp Noibmys."

ORBIT
Melinda Beck created this image for the song "(Love Theme From) Concourse A."

CATHODE [top]
The song "Long Pig" inspired Bob Maloney to design this image.

MARGO Vs. THUNDERBALL
Vida Russell came up with this design for the song "Let Everything Be."

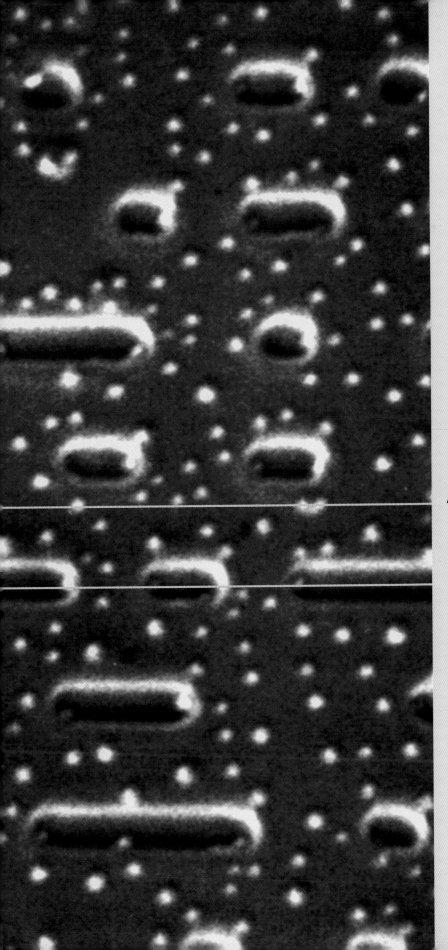

3
ATMOSPHERE

Atmosphere addresses designers'
interpretations of musical movement
in space and change over time.
Some examples have a fixed
beginning, middle and end, as in
a musical score, while others are
more abstract in structure and context.
Visual and musical juxtapositions
and syntheses, and visual forms
that have no direct relationship with
music except in time and/or space,
are explored.

LIQUID SOUND

Glenn McKay's legendary career began in the 1960s in San Francisco, following an extensive experimentation with psychoactive drugs. After a visit to one of the Acid Tests (wild concerts organized by Ken Kesey) at the Fillmore Auditorium, where McKay saw his first light show, he launched what would become a journey of artistic innovation lasting over thirty-five years. Collaborations with such major music artists as Jefferson Airplane and Grateful Dead have given McKay—trained as a painter—unmatched notoriety in the unique art of the light show. McKay describes himself as an architect of emotions, "I'm providing a new door to the consciousness of sound and color . . . [so that one is] in touch with the emotion and the rhythm of the experience and loses any sense of separation between the color, moving images and the sound."

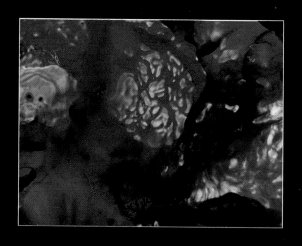

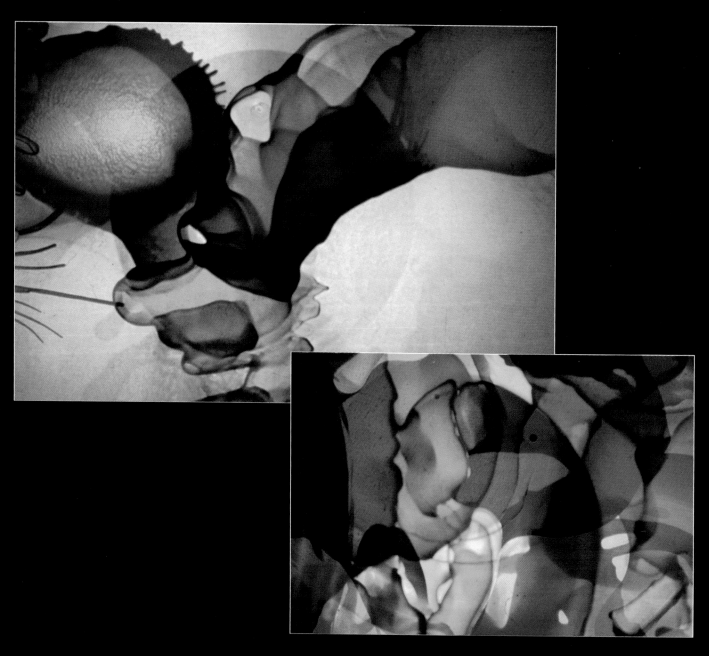

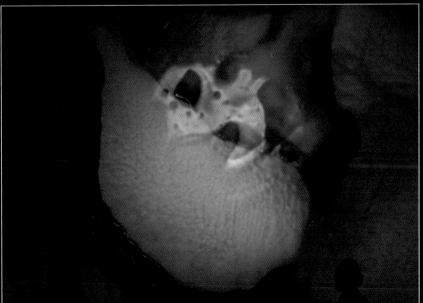

McKay creates what are known as oil-dish projections. His media is light, which he focuses on a rear-projection screen in auditoriums and other venues. McKay's arsenal of creative tools includes two overhead projectors, four color wheels, four dissolve units and a library containing thousands of hand-painted slides.

The light shows must be experienced live. McKay visualizes the inner experience of music with liquefied textures, intense colors and pulsating patterns that resonate with the audience long after the last note is played.

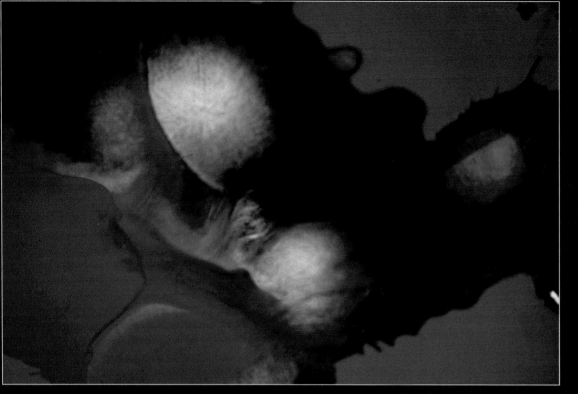

McKay's art is consistently evolving. He works with a variety of contemporary music, ranging from African drums to jazz to ambient electronic music.

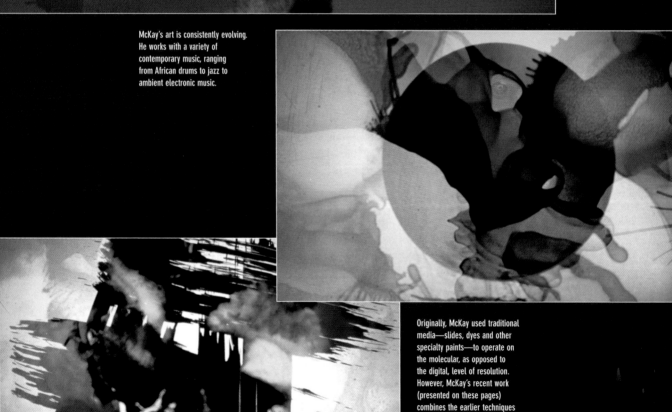

Originally, McKay used traditional media—slides, dyes and other specialty paints—to operate on the molecular, as opposed to the digital, level of resolution. However, McKay's recent work (presented on these pages) combines the earlier techniques with the digital. The artist imports his hand-painted slides into an electronic environment and edits his creations on video tape.

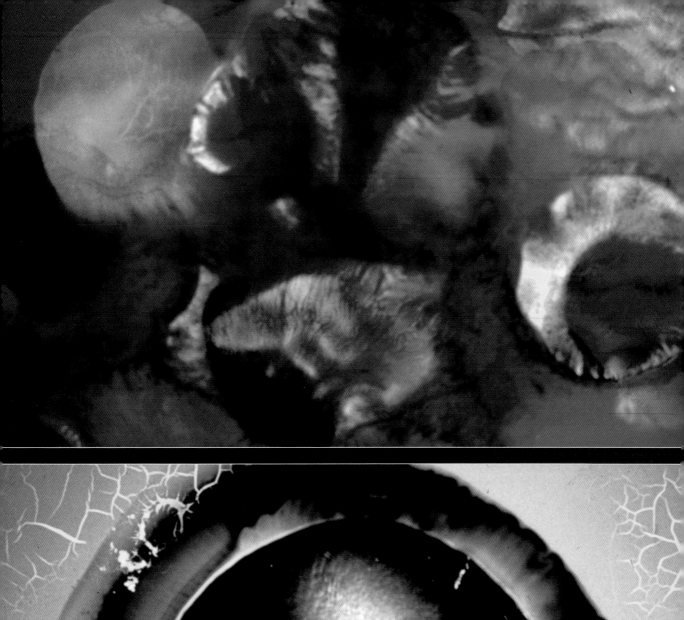
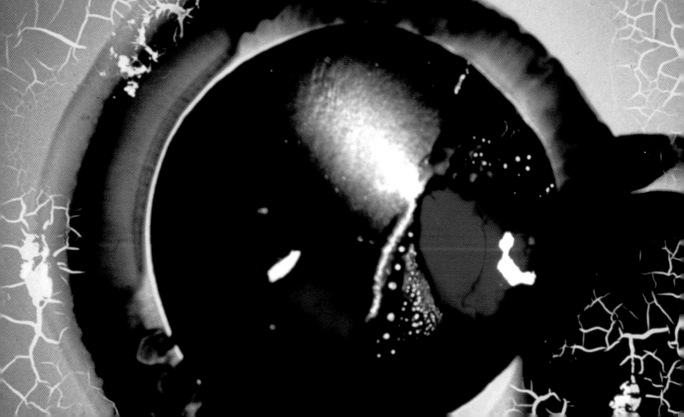

VISUAL RAPTURE

In recent years, Paul Sych, designer and jazz musician, has focused his design and typography on a distinct and personalized vision. His curiosity, suspicion and trepidation about design are the driving forces behind the manifestation of his emotions on paper. As a jazz musician, Sych finds unique inspiration in his musical peers, and he strives to isolate the spirit of their self-expression and to understand the methods by which they create their individual artistic voice.

It has been a difficult process for Sych to bridge the parallels between the musical and the visual arts, but at the same time it has represented an exciting challenge for him.

Sych has generated a body of work that is entirely personal and unbridled by rules or commercial considerations. It is not simply a demonstration of technical and creative artifice.

ETHEREAL PULSES

Ying Tan, associate professor of the Department of Arts at the University of Oregon, started out as a Chinese landscape painter. For many years, however, she has been working with digital media to explore creative ideas. After mastering 3-D computer-animation skills, Tan's focus shifted from professional design to experimental work. This new direction reveals an interest in non-narrative, abstract visual expression in computer animation and digital imaging. Tan's on-going projects are based on the animation of musical compositions and her work has been shown nationally and internationally.

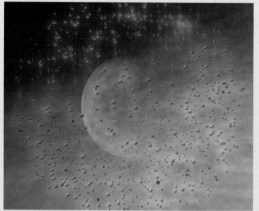

The strengths of digital imaging and computer animation lie in their ability to synthesize experimentation, layering, replication and unexpected visual forms. Tan employs simple geometric structures, soft-edged 3-D illusions and slowly evolving atmospheric effects, to generate a poetic visual experience that responds to or echoes the music. Tan moves away from the rigid sleekness of high-tech computer rendering and embraces a flowing painterly sensation.

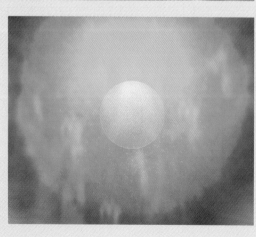

ELEMENTS IN TRANSFORMATION, no. 1, 1998

Duration: 1.00 minute

Short sequences show the symbolic systems of the cosmos and the evolution and transformation of elemental forms. Circles and spheres appear as individual entities, as well as parts that form the whole. For Tan, these elements symbolize the oneness of body and spirit, the oneness of man's inner and outer worlds.

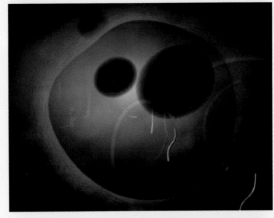

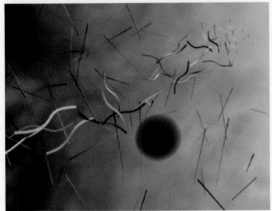

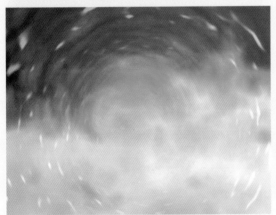

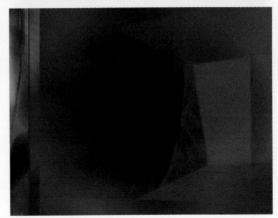

UN ALBOR (DAWN), 1999

Duration: 3.40 minutes

Tan created an experimental animation to accompany a composition by Jeffrey Stolet (1955–), which is based on a poem by the Spaniard Gustava Adolfo Becquer (1836–70). Becquer's brief verses appear to be autobiographical, yet blend fantasy and reality with a vivid sense of color and vagueness. The poem on which "Un Albor" is based, starts with a magnificent break of dawn, continues along a splendid external landscape and ends in the dark night of a human soul wondering whether dawn will ever come. Stolet's score is rich in emotion, with haunting digital sound effects. Tan portrays the music and the poem with abstract forms that are vivid and sublime.

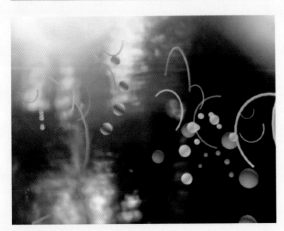

ELEMENTS IN TRANSFORMATION, no. 2, 1998
Duration: 1.50 minutes

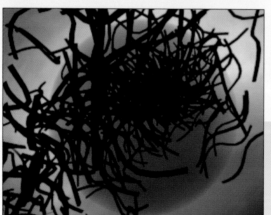

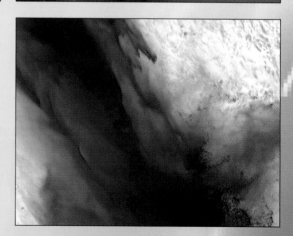

UNDERNEATH
THE BUNKER

It is perhaps Jakob Brandt-Pedersen's passion for composing music and performance pieces—which he has done for ten years—that plays the most pivotal role in his success, despite his education as a graphic designer. His most recent work focuses on the relationship between music and image, resulting in a series of interactive CD-ROMs.

<u>Bunker</u> generates abstract graphics in response to the music of the Kom De Bagfra Orchestra, a three-member group. The experience is inspired by the atmospheric west coast of Brandt-Pedersen's native Denmark, where the beautiful and sometimes harsh natural landscape is interrupted by eroded concrete bunkers from World War II. <u>Levana</u>, a double CD, consists of twelve virtual worlds that the user explores while listening to music by the Kom De Bagfra Orchestra.

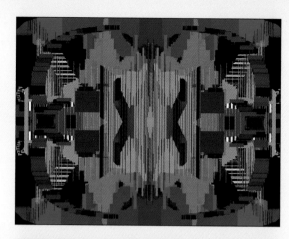

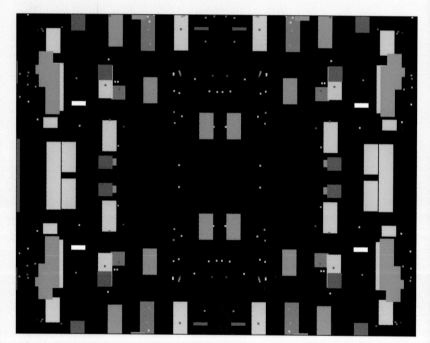

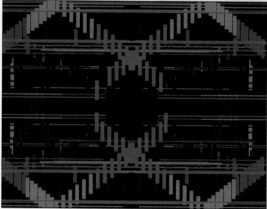

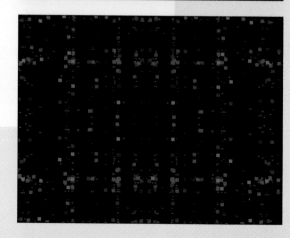

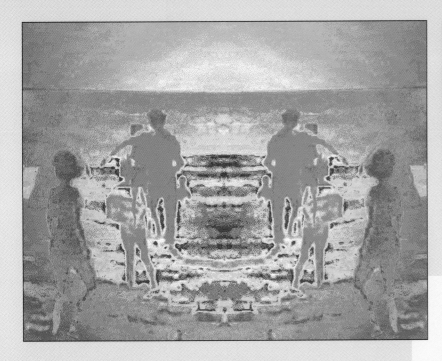

The Kom De Bagfra Orchestra created twenty-five hours of improvised synthesizer music. Brandt-Pedersen noticed that there was a dark and unpleasant side to many of the recordings. Suddenly the synthesizers sounded like bomber planes on a night trip to dump their deadly load on a designated target during World War II.

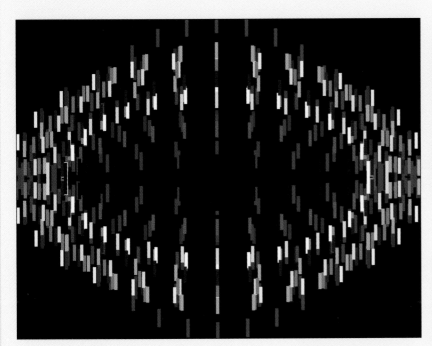

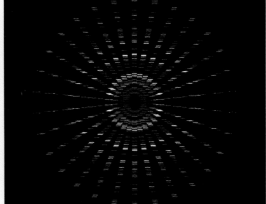

Brandt-Pedersen mixed the pieces together to tell an abstract story. Starting with the beach, the sea and the dunes, the journey leads to the bunkers. It finishes back at the beach.

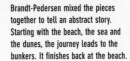

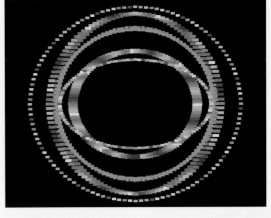

To further visualize the story, Brandt-Pedersen developed a computer program in MAX—an interactive MIDI environment. It opens with shots of the sea and bunkers, but as the music evolves, the software starts generating its own graphics. The results are always different to encourage the viewer to experience the same kind of travels as Brandt-Pedersen when he compiled the music.

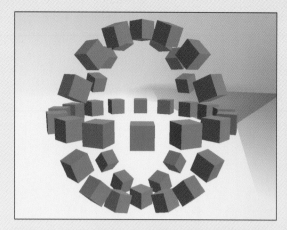

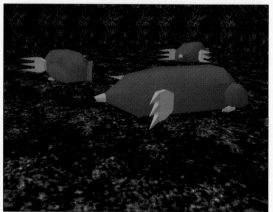

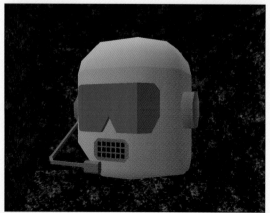

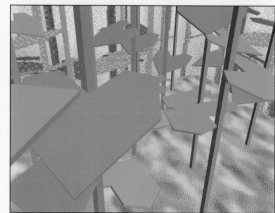

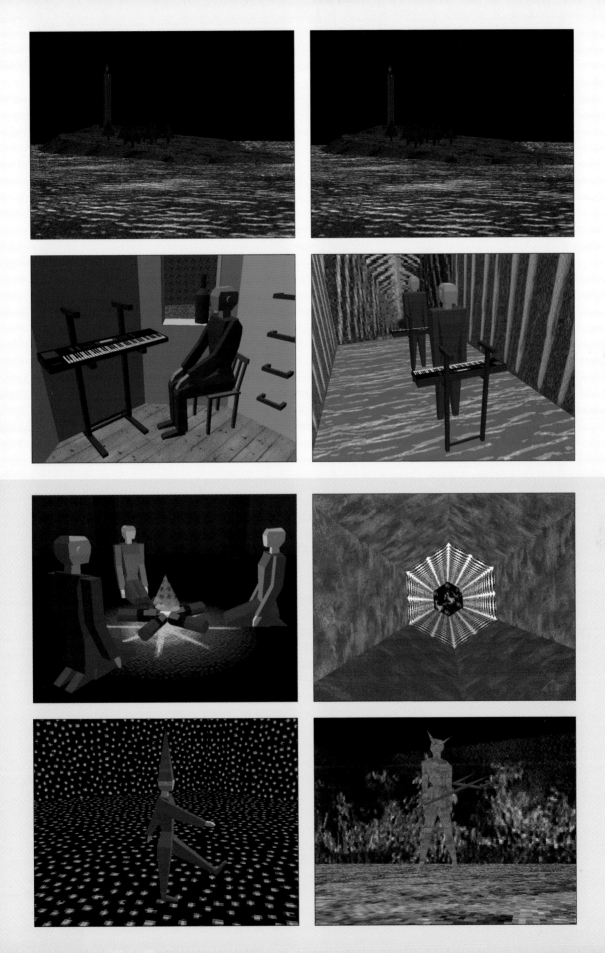

STATIC AND HISS

Video artist Dan Mahoney is greatly intrigued by the possibilities of video feedback and image generation. He has always been interested in abstract art, and thought that the next stage in its evolution was to make the image move and emit sound. Mahoney believes that video feedback is similar to life itself: It is "seeded," it "grows" and it "dies." Many of the complex effects in Mahoney's work are produced from such simple shapes as triangles and circles. Video feedback is a strange and beautiful process, and Mahoney feels that he has only scratched the surface of what is attainable.

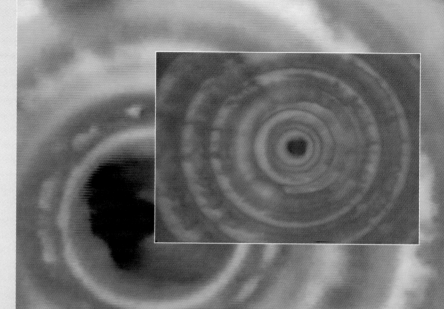

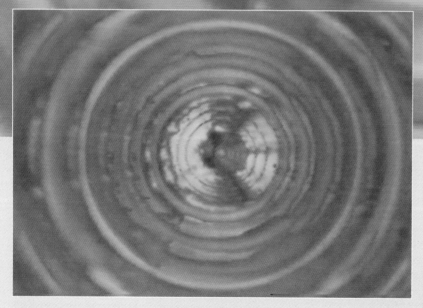

FEEDBACK
Video feedback, in its simplest form, consists of pointing a camera at a television monitor that is displaying the camera's image. This process results in the repeated pattern of one monitor inside another, inside another, etc. When one zooms into the monitor, a flowing pattern is created, and if the camera is tilted, each successive image will also be at the same angle.

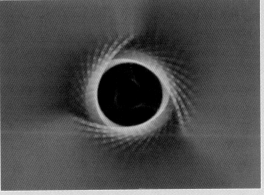

FORMATIONS
The resolution is low and the ability to control the feedback is limited. Therefore, Mahoney uses a DVE (digital video effects) box, which acts as the camera and the monitor. The repeating feedback patterns are clearer and more precise, with extremely smooth zooms, pans and rotations.

SONIC SCULPTURE

Dennis Miller received his doctorate in music composition from Columbia University in 1981. Since then he has worked in the music faculty of Northeastern University in Boston, where he heads the music technology program and chairs the Multimedia Studies Steering Committee.

The League–ISCM is a music organization created by modern composers who felt that they needed to form an "advocacy group" in order to present their work effectively to the public. Miller was the founder of the League–ISCM in Boston, and served as its director from 1982 until 1988. He began his career as a graphic artist and animator in 1997, and his work has been presented worldwide.

Miller's work brings recognizable shapes and icons into the virtual world. He is particularly interested in creating highly colored images that display repeated patterns of movement, similar to the rhythmic patterns often found in his musical compositions.

The digital images are created on the POVray scene description application, a public-domain programming language.

LISTENING TO CHAOS

Post Tool Design, a California-based partnership, was formed in 1993 by David Karam and Gigi Biederman. They specialize "in the strange and the beautiful" and their multimedia products feature surreal characters, organic objects, 3-D letterforms and other-worldly color palettes.

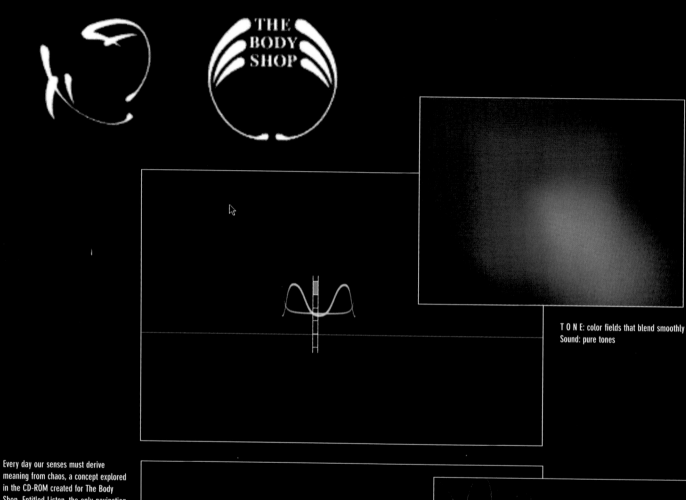

T O N E: color fields that blend smoothly
Sound: pure tones

Every day our senses must derive meaning from chaos, a concept explored in the CD-ROM created for The Body Shop. Entitled Listen, the only navigation tool is a sine wave, activated by the click of a computer mouse. Once in view, the wave may be altered in size and position, to correspond to a range of states from chaos to meditation.

The user must listen to the piece and the piece must listen to the user; they are continually updating each other. Once the user physiologically filters out the noise and adjusts to the language, he or she can cognitively comprehend the content. However, the continuum never rests and the user must adapt to interactive drifting.

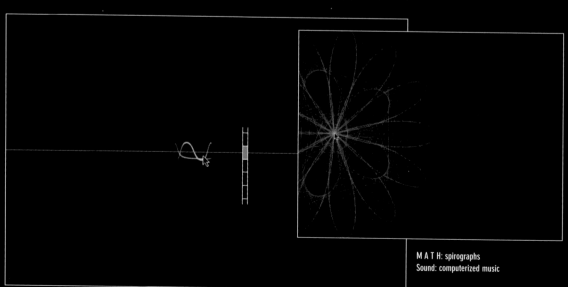

M A T H: spirographs
Sound: computerized music

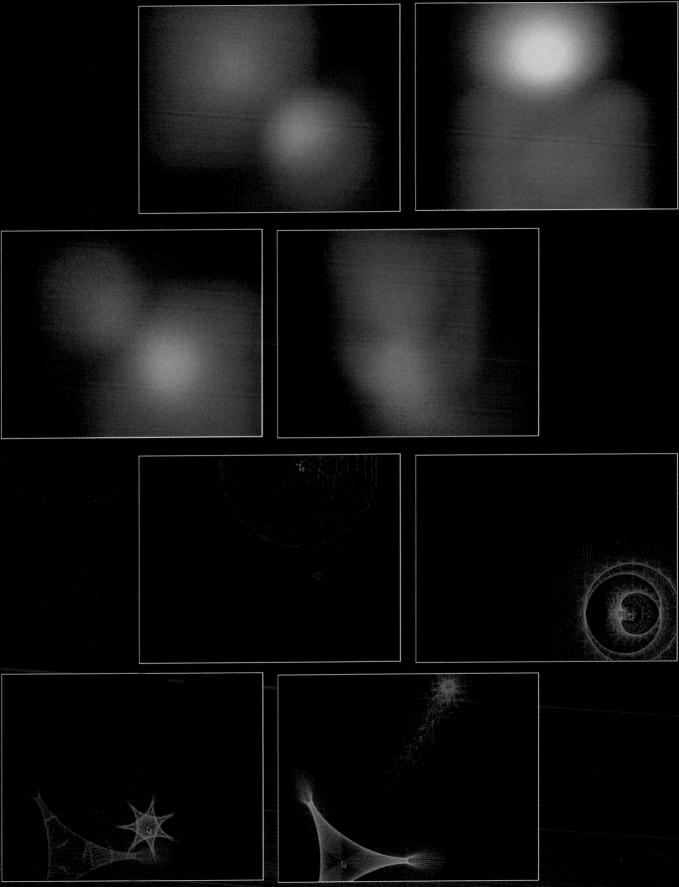

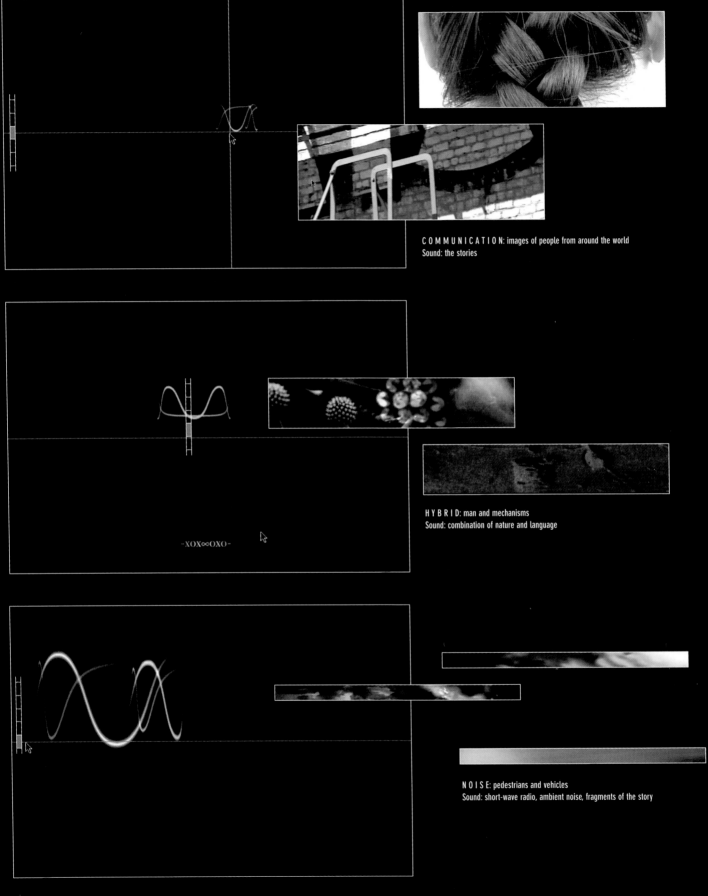

C O M M U N I C A T I O N: images of people from around the world
Sound: the stories

H Y B R I D: man and mechanisms
Sound: combination of nature and language

-XOX∞OXO-

N O I S E: pedestrians and vehicles
Sound: short-wave radio, ambient noise, fragments of the story

COMMUNICATION

A list of stories, recited in several
languages, addresses such topics as
hospitality, human affairs, the senses
and language. Series of images are
revealed as each story is told.

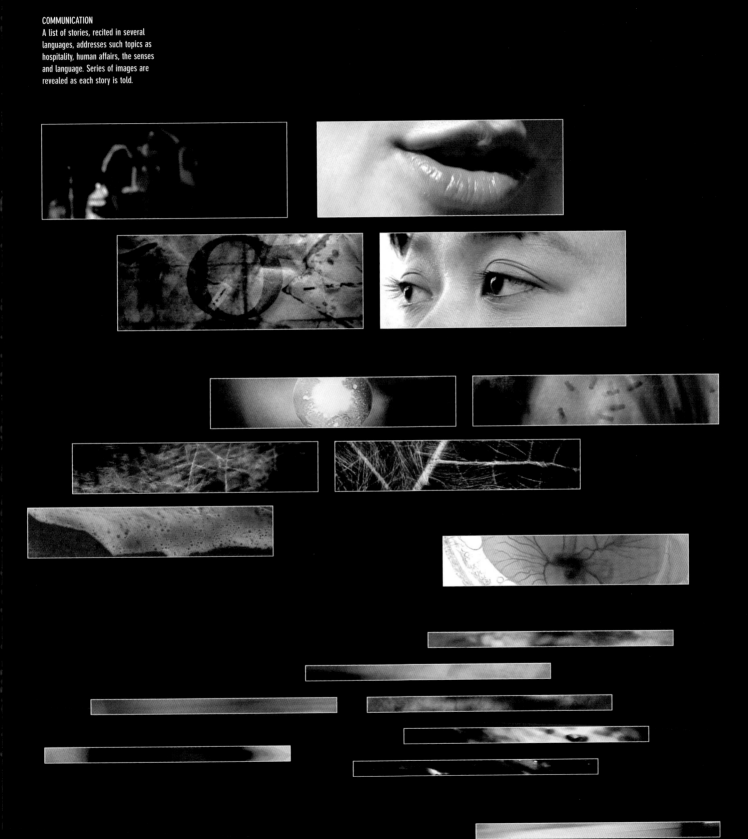

NOCTURNAL EMISSIONS

Nocturne is a series of short experimental films, in which artist Sheri Wills pursues a visual translation of Victorian music. The hallmark of her work lies in its tightly laced obsession with detail and decoration, decorum and charm. The sound is subdued and repetitive, while the images are redolent and florid. The music that inspired much of the series is Mendelssohn's oratorio Elijah, although there are no specific references to it in the films.

NOCTURNE 1 AND 2
Created through an interweaving of traditional film-making techniques and computer technology, the films are a series of stiffly animated scenes of flower patterns. They move in minute increments to reveal glimpses of the figurative painting in the background. Each scene is marked by the iris of the lens darkening the outer perimeter of the frame, an effect associated with early cinema. Similar to cut-out animation, films tick by with the rhythmic sense of a machine, as the decorative patterns change bit by bit.

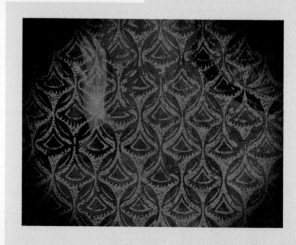

The registration between images is necessarily imperfect. While this might be considered detrimental to most animated films, it is an effect the artist desires in this work. Each individual image moves, for instance, from side to side, up and down or even diagonally. The rhythmic jerkiness acts as a metronome and forms the underlying structure and the primary characteristic of the films. The movement is awkward and, in combination with the silhouetted forms, lends an overall effect reminiscent of shadow puppets. It is the idiosyncrasy of the movement that makes the films appear handmade, even though all images were created on computer.

AURAL PLASTICITY

"Organizing synthetic sounds according to the conventional principles of Western music is generally quite problematic; in order to compose with synthetic sounds a different approach must be sought. A possible approach may be to use features taken from visual language and apply them to the aural domain. If it is possible to establish links between aural and visual events, then visual language can help create a synthetic-sound composition, as well as an audiovisual piece."
Adriano Abbado, 1999

Artist and musician Adriano Abbado establishes links between perceptual categories of synthetic sounds and abstract visual forms. He considers different areas of application chiefly through the creation of a new type of audiovisual work that focuses on the interaction between aural and visual "objects," rather than between music and images. The method he proposes is formed around visual language and leads to a new way of composing and thinking about music based on timbres or tone qualities. Featured on these pages are visual works and excerpts from Abbado's M.I.T. thesis.

SOUND AS OBJECT
A series of computer-generated visual manifestations of sound are presented on these pages. The work displays an ethereal quality that is at once material and immaterial.

SPACE
Certain modern composers pay great attention to the arrangement of instruments in space and to the spatial pattern that sounds follow. The reason for this is that, at the cerebral level, there is only one organ that receives signals from both the ears and the eyes: the colliculus superior. It can thus be described as the only audiovisual part of the human body.

The colliculus superior is responsible for the spatial positioning of aural and visual events. In other words, there is a mapping between the position of a signal and the cells devoted to its processing. These cells are activated by both a visual and an aural stimulus. If two signals (one visual, one aural) are perceived from the same point in space, the group of cells will react more intensely. This demonstrates that the spatial perception of an audiovisual event departs from an objective base.

It is necessary to emphasize that the sensitivity of the ear (and that of the entire hearing system) to spatial movements is inferior compared to its sensitivity to sound frequency or intensity. In the realm of spatial perception, the lateral movements of a sound are more easily picked up than the vertical ones. The spectral content or timbre of a sound is best detected spatially if there are many high frequencies.

Consequently, the dimension of a visual object (that is depicting an aural object) depends on the spectral content of the associated sound, for example, a sound that is fundamentally low will be associated with a big visual object. A low sound does not have a precise position in space and is spread out, while a high sound is small because it is more easily located in space.

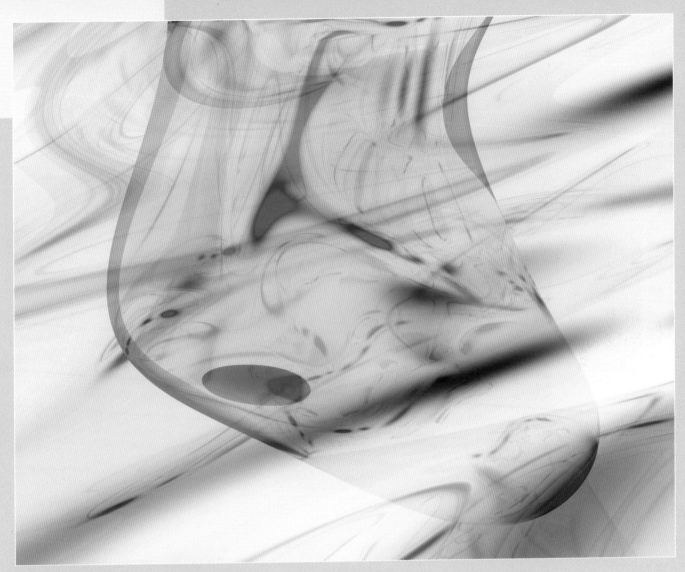

INTENSITY

The contrast between an object, whether visual or aural, and the intensity of the background noise is important. There are situations where it is not possible to distinguish clearly an object from its background noise, and sometimes there is a complete fusion.

SHAPE, COLOR and TIMBRE

An abstract object, aural or visual, is inherently difficult to define because there is no precise terminology. For instance, a sound could be described as "brilliant," but how does one visualize such a sound? One could use an object that is bright and shiny and has its own internal brilliance, a phenomenon that would be more evident in the presence of other less bright objects.

However, another difficulty is the shape of the object. Consider for a moment a "non-brilliant" sound. This type of sound does not contain high frequencies and would be represented by a shape with little detail. Therefore, a brilliant sound would be portrayed by a form with a highly detailed texture, full of small signs.

Evidence shows that a curve suggests continuity and is associated with a low frequency, while edges indicate a higher frequency. Therefore, a brilliant sound will be an acute visual object with many details and edges.

TIME

Sounds change over time, that is, their spectral content is dynamic. The representation of a visual object shows a parallel development with the passing of time.

If one were to imagine a violin sound, a picture of a violin would probably come to mind. However, no mental model is evoked by the concept of an electronic sound. It is, therefore, most useful to define such ideas in everyday language, using adjectives like shiny, bright, dull and metallic. Other common attributes of the musical world are borrowed from Latin, for example, allegro, presto, and so on.

PAINTING WITH SOUND

Second Story has created interactive experiences delivered via the Web and other media since 1994. The studio blends technology and storytelling on such topics as adventure travel, architecture, music, photography and history. Second Story's projects have been recognized in almost every major interactive design competition and in dozens of books and magazines. In 1999, the company was awarded the annual Communication Arts interactive design award for the fifth time. Its work has also been included in the Smithsonian's permanent research collection on information technology at the National Museum of American History.

FOREST FOR THE TREES

Second Story was hired by DreamWorks Records to create a promotional website for the album Forest for the Trees, the brainchild of singer, songwriter and producer Carl Stephenson. Stephenson's organic collage of hip-hop beats and psychedelic textures uses instruments from guitar and keyboards to sitar, bagpipes and didgeridoo.

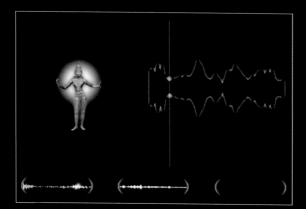

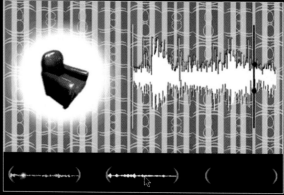

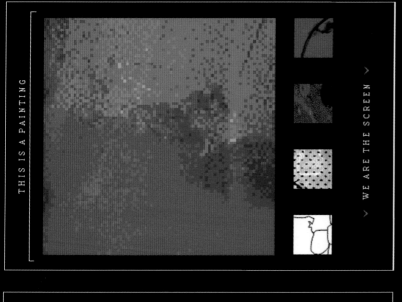

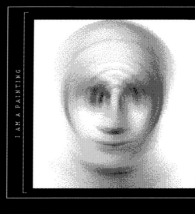

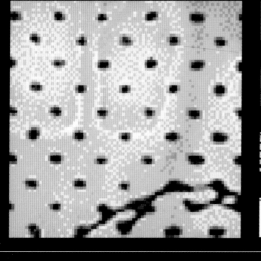

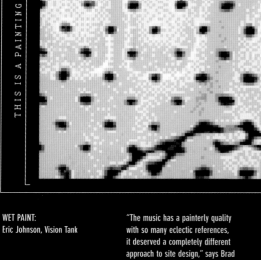

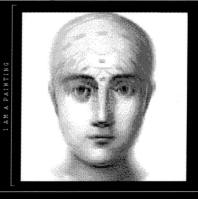

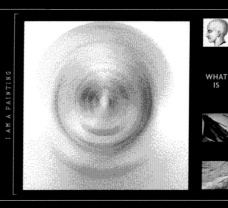

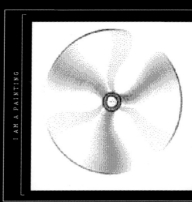

WET PAINT:
Eric Johnson, Vision Tank

"The music has a painterly quality
with so many eclectic references,
it deserved a completely different
approach to site design," says Brad
Johnson, partner in Second Story.
"Each track is so unique and varied that
a single design treatment for the whole
album would be a compromise—
it might approximate each song,
but wouldn't really fit any of them."

click the tree
to begin

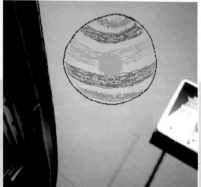

navigation

contemplation

YOU CREATE THE REASON: Aufuldish & Warinner Borrowing from the phrase "You can't see the forest for the trees," Second Story made the project a collaborative effort between different designers, who each focused on one song. Bob Aufuldish and Kathy Warinner, Amy Franceschini, Brad Johnson and Eric Johnson each picked a track from the album. The artists then produced "something interactive" that included loops or samples from the track. Each participant was unaware of the other's contribution until the end. The result was a "forest of trees," a testament to the musical inspiration of <u>Forest for the Trees</u>.

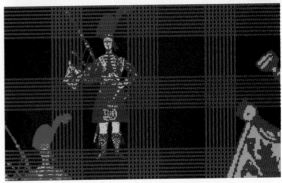

DREAM: Brad Johnson, Second Story

ENTRANCING INTERFACE

Artist Lee Roskin works on what he terms musical light shows, which simultaneously use computers, peripheral devices and several pieces of video and audio equipment. Roskin's goal is to make a live performance of lights, colors and shapes that respond to music as it is played. He refers to his video productions as a Jackson Pollock painting set to music. The visuals are not generated from paint dripped onto a canvas, but by light emanating from a video monitor or projector. Roskin has recorded his shows on a collection of videos (Music Visions) that attempt to bring together modern music and visual art. The images on these pages appear in his light shows, but also stand by themselves as music that has been freeze-framed for the eye.

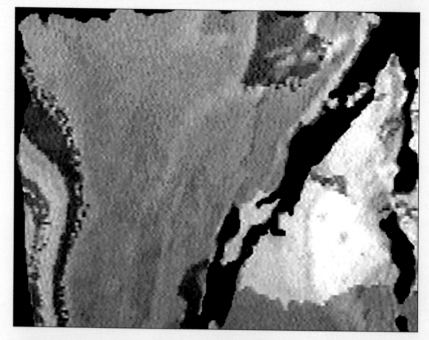

  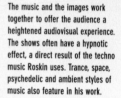

The music and the images work together to offer the audience a heightened audiovisual experience. The shows often have a hypnotic effect, a direct result of the techno music Roskin uses. Trance, space, psychedelic and ambient styles of music also feature in his work.

 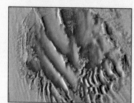 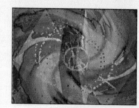

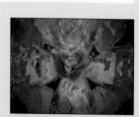

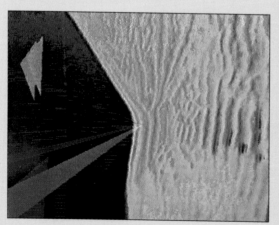

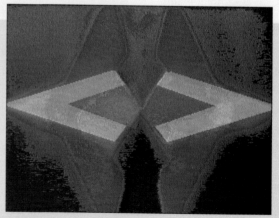

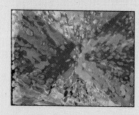

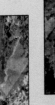

In Roskin's system, the human operator is considered the interface between the music and the visuals, changing the many controls to determine the overall combination and effect.

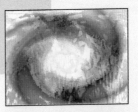

A hardware device captures the music and sends the data (in real time) to the computer, where the software makes a moving display of colors, objects, patterns and pictures in response to the music and under the control of the operator.

Roskin controls the many parameters of the light show. These include the colors and special effects on the video digitizer, the camera (focus, exposure, zoom, shutter speed) and the dissolve/luminance option on the mixer. There are many controls and little time to plan what to do next, so after a few seconds of preparation, intuition takes over and guides each show.

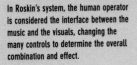

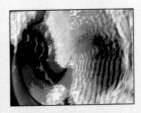

SENSORY OVERLOAD

Elliott Peter Earls graduated from Cranbrook Academy of Art. He is founder of The Apollo Program, an experimental media studio, type foundry and design firm, with a list of clients in the music and publishing industries. Earls constantly pushes the limits of digital technology for purely investigative and creative ends. His CD-ROM <u>Throwing Apples at the Sun</u> features a complex and unpredictable interactive experience involving multiple layers of type, image, motion and sound. Earls's celebrated poster series promoting his typeface designs demonstrates how even the traditionally static medium of 2-D design can become a kinetic, 3-D and sonic experience.

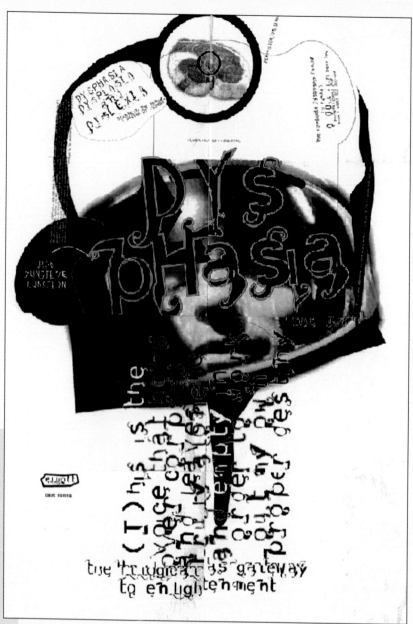

· Typeface: DYSPHASIA

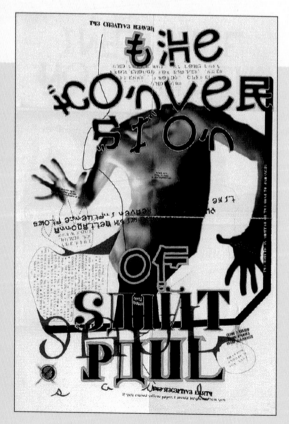

Typeface: SAINT PAUL

THE APOLLO PROGRAM
The posters on these pages were created by Earls to promote his type foundry. Their dynamic collisions of word and image make Earls's work instantly recognizable. His multimedia live performances are becoming known worldwide.

THROWING APPLES AT THE SUN
The CD-ROM contains a collection of sounds, images, words and motion graphics. A simple click of the computer mouse on any area of the poster will instigate a journey through a vast repertoire of sounds and images.

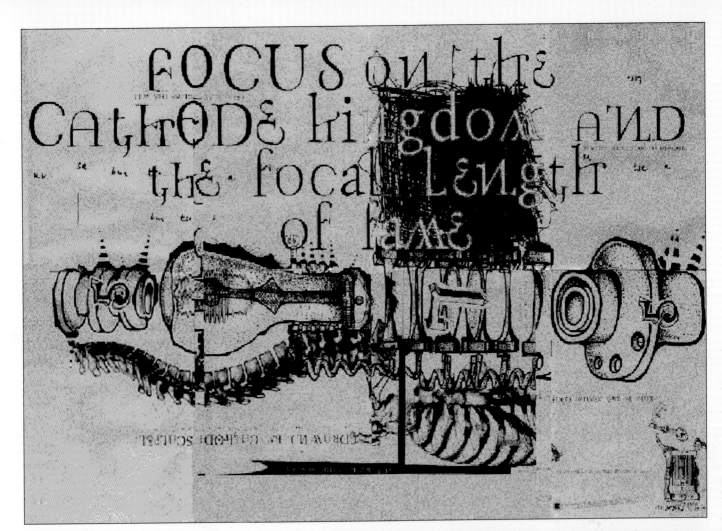

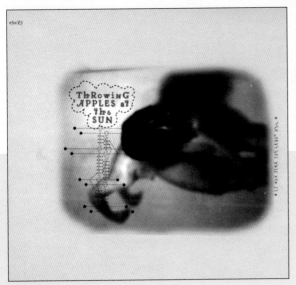

CD-ROM cover

AUDIO DIAGRAM
An illustrated guide to Earls's
equipment list for <u>Throwing Apples
at the Sun</u>.

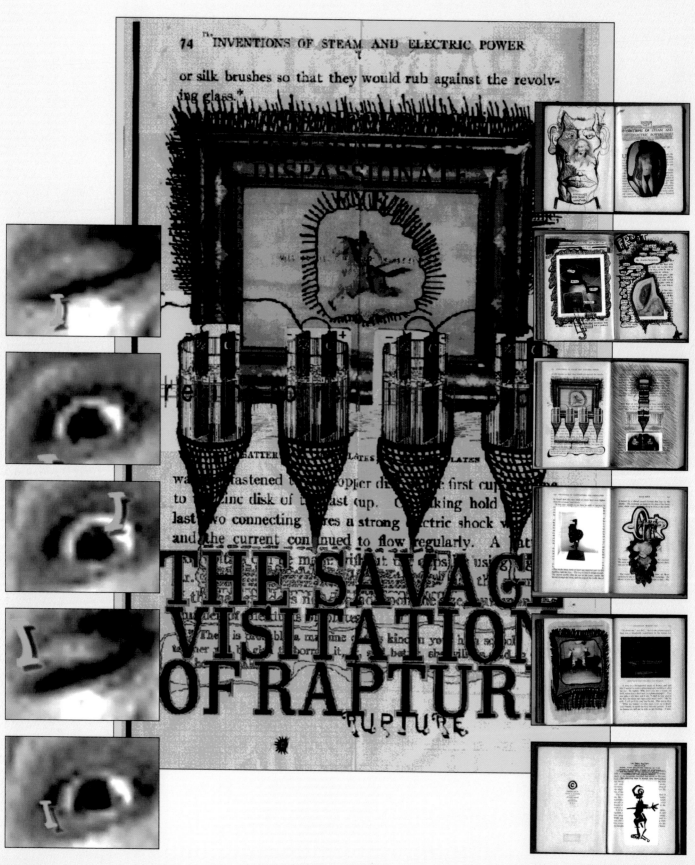

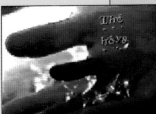

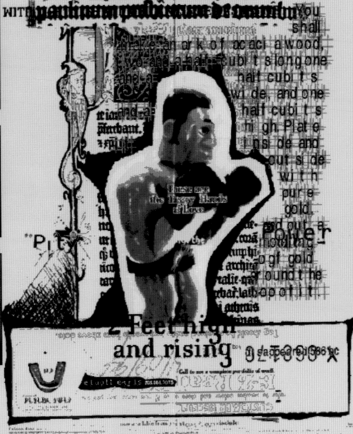

PAINFULLY
BOXING
GABRIEL

Samples of what the viewer may encounter on <u>Throwing Apples at the Sun</u>.

AURAL MUTATIONS

Akira Rabelais considers himself a composer who writes software, not an engineer who makes music. Drawing on rich literary sources, West Coast–based Rabelais has been writing sound and graphics software and recording his own music—with tutelage from such electroacoustical legends as Tom Erbe and Larry Polansky—since 1990. The result, Argeïphontes Lyre (AL), is a family of software programs that allows the user to transform specific sounds, images and computer file names into unpredictable patterns.

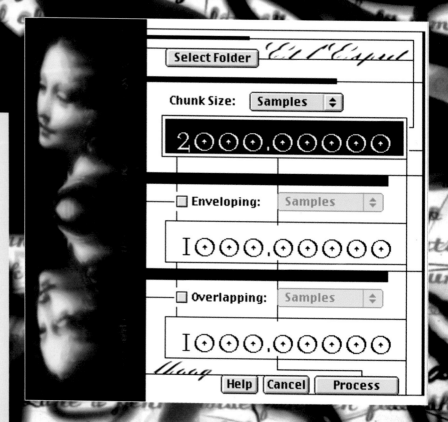

AL's various functions, which have complex mathematical algorithms at their root, have been assigned such names as Dynamic FM Synthesis, Time Domain Mutation, Morphological Disintegration and Eviscerator Reanimator. They are best described as tools that pound, shred, cut, pull, push and glue digital information— the language of the computer— into sonic narratives.

Time Domain Mutation, for example, introduces two separate sound files in a manner determined by the user. This meeting can range from cordial to hostile to unpredictable. However, the result is always a mutant. Rabelais explains, "Consider two sandwiches:

a grilled jalapeno and tofu on wheat, and a peanut butter and jelly on rye. If you wanted to apply a mutation algorithm to the sandwiches, you would first select one as the source— let's say the jalapeno—and the other—the peanut butter—as the target. Now start analysing the sandwiches. You get a hot and squishy bit from the source and a sweet sticky bit from the target. Depending on the type of mutation you're using, you might come up with something like hot-sticky or squishy-sweet. That new bit could end up in your new sandwich—the restaurant mutant— or it might not, because there is a certain amount of random chance in the process."

Select Source | Select Target | Help | Cancel | Process

Type: USIM

Absolute Interval: Use Function

Mutation Index (Ω): ⊙.5⊙3676

Delta Emphasis (-1 -> 1): ⊙.⊙⊙43⊙

Set
Reverse
Invert
Shift H
Shift V
Smooth

Cycles ⊙.75

This module looks for up to 2⊙⊙
The files are opened and the given (h
is read sequentially from each and u

1 - 9999   2 - 1⊙⊙⊙⊙
1   1⊙⊙⊙⊙

Help | Cancel | Process

Mod Wave | Car Wave
Car Wave -32768 -> 32767
⊙.433824
Duration
1⊙.4682

Fm | Fc
Index
Exponential
Distortion
Set
Reverse
Invert
Shift H
Shift V
Smooth

Car Amp

Fc:Fm Ratio

Cycles 4.23

Select First File | Select Second File

Consider String   irregular
unsigned

Curiouser and curiouser!

Help | Cancel | Process

Select First File | Select Second File

process Aposiopesis Modulation

Shift 1 -> 15
⊙.192315516821I845

Larger Values 0 -> 100   Smaller Values 0 -> 100
8⊙⊙.⊙   83.17

Help | Cancel | Process

Rabelais cites Tom Erb's SoundHack
mutation program and Larry Polansky's
utilities for synthesizing two sound
files as inspiration for AL.
The program has been embraced
by such electronics companies as
Scanner and Terre Thaemlitz who use
it to structure sound samples. Rabelais
has assembled his own compositions
on a CD called Elongated
Pentagonal Pyramid.

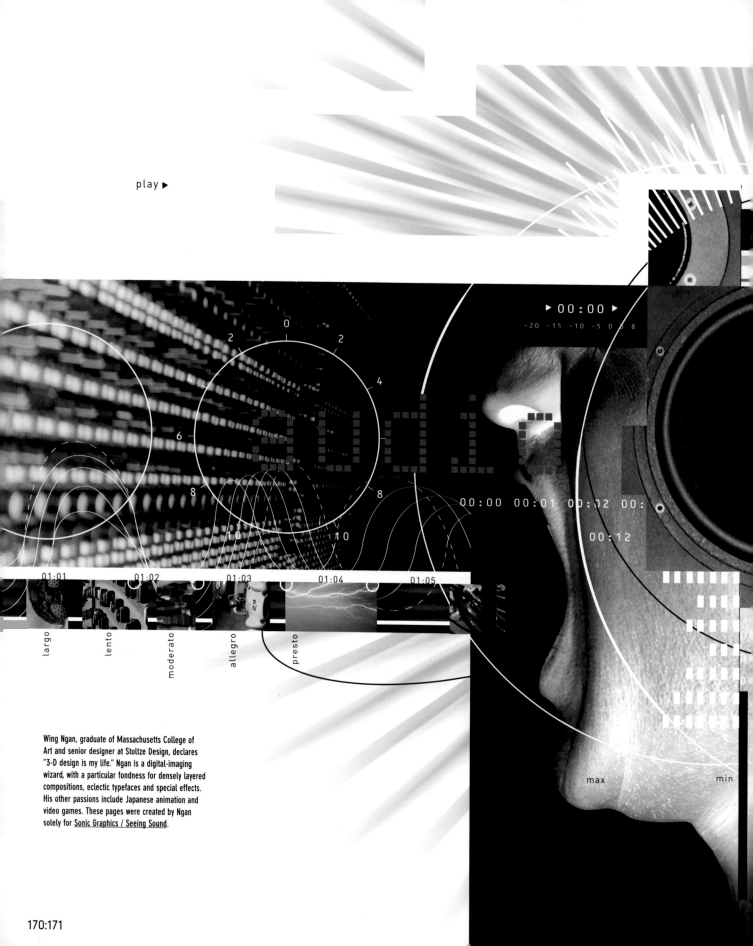

play ▶

▶ 00:00 ▶
-20 -15 -10 -5 0 3 8

0
2   2
4   4
6
8   8
10   10

00:00 00:01 00:02 00:
00:12

01:01   01:02   01:03   01:04   01:05

largo   lento   moderato   allegro   presto

max   min

Wing Ngan, graduate of Massachusetts College of
Art and senior designer at Stoltze Design, declares
"3-D design is my life." Ngan is a digital-imaging
wizard, with a particular fondness for densely layered
compositions, eclectic typefaces and special effects.
His other passions include Japanese animation and
video games. These pages were created by Ngan
solely for Sonic Graphics / Seeing Sound.

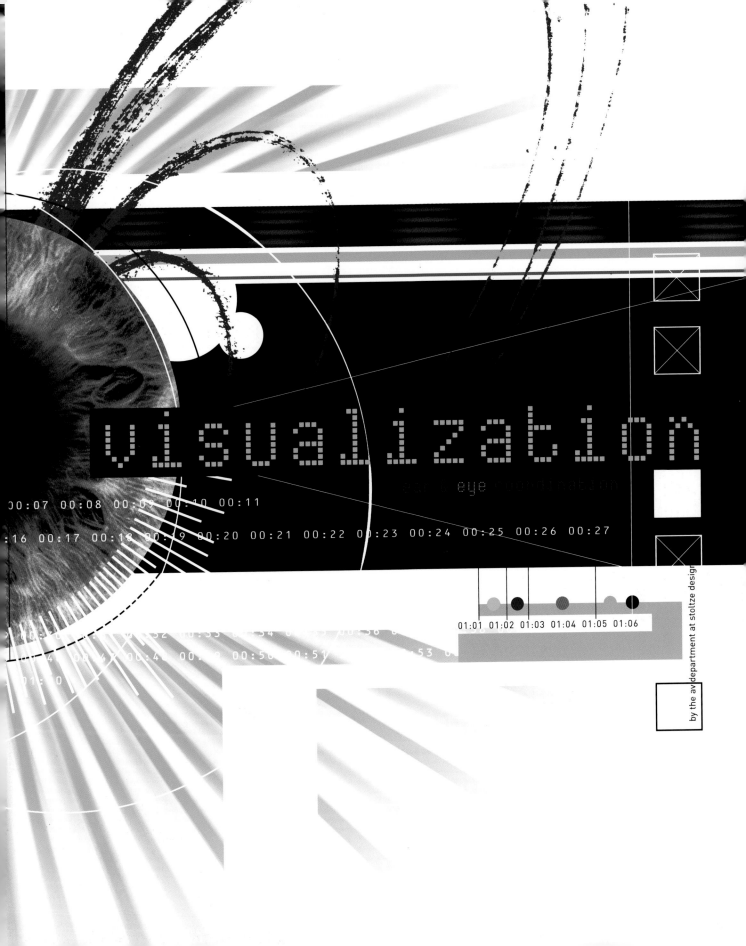

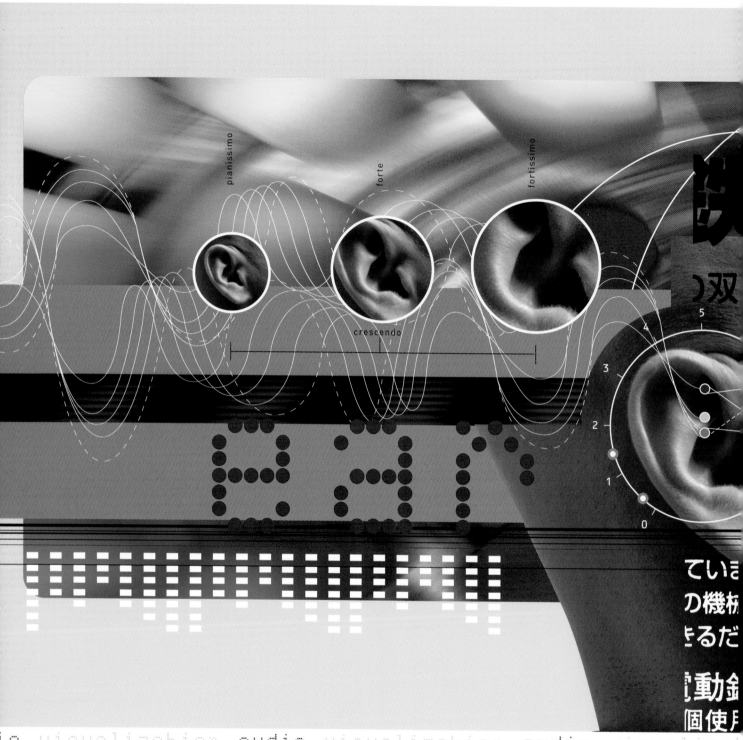

BIBLIOGRAPHY

Antokoletz, Elliott. Twentieth Century Music. Englewood Cliffs, N. J.: Prentice Hall, 1992.

Barthes, Roland. Image · Music · Text. Translated by Stephen Heath. New York: Hill & Wang, 1977.

Blackwell, Lewis. David Carson, 2nd Sight: Grafik Design after the End of Print. New York: St Martin's Press, 1997.

————. The End of Print: The Graphic Design of David Carson. San Francisco: Chronicle Books, 1996.

Blink. Fly: The Art of the Club Flyer. London: Thames & Hudson Ltd, New York: Watson-Guptill Publications, 1996.

Cage, John. Silence. Middletown, CT: Wesleyan University Press, 1973.

————. Notations. New York: Something Else Press, 1969.

Cage, John, and Joan Retallack. Musicage: Cage Muses on Words, Art, Music. Middletown, CT: Wesleyan University Press, 1997.

Cope, David. New Directions in Music. 6th ed. Dubuque, Iowa: William C. Brown Communications Inc, 1993.

Cytowic, Richard E., M.D. The Man Who Tasted Shapes: A Bizarre Medical Mystery Offers Revolutionary Insights into Emotions, Reasoning, and Consciousness. New York: G. P. Putnam's Sons, 1993.

Cummings, David (ed). Random House Encyclopedic History of Classical Music. New York: Random House, 1997.

Dann, Kevin. Bright Colors Falsely Seen. New Haven: Yale University Press, 1999.

Düchting, Hajo. Paul Klee: Painting and Music. New York: Prestel-Verlag, 1997.

Eagle, Mary. Virtual Reality. National Gallery of Australia, 1995.

ECM: Sleeves of Desire: A Cover Story. Switzerland: Lars Müller Publishers, 1996.

Hiebert, Kenneth J. Graphic Design Sources. New Haven: Yale University Press, 1998.

Jenny, Hans. Cymatics. Basel: Basilius Presse AG, 1967.

Johnson, Heather. Roy De Maistre: The English Years, 1930–1968.

Kagan, Andrew. Paul Klee: Art & Music. Ithaca, NY: Cornell University Press, 1983.

Kandinsky, Vasily. Point and Line to Plane. New York: Dover Publications Inc, 1979.

————. Concerning the Spiritual in Art. New York: Dover Publications Inc, 1977.

Klanten, Robert (ed). BüroDestruct. Berlin: Die Gestalten Verlag, 1999.

Kostelanetx, Richard. John Cage (Ex)plain(ed). New York: Schirmer Books, 1996.

Kuipers, Dean. RayGun: Out of Control. New York: Simon & Schuster, 1997.

Langer, Susan K. Mind: An Essay on Human Feelings.

McDonough, Jack. San Francisco Rock: The Illustrated History of San Francisco Rock Music. San Francisco: Chronicle Books, 1985.

Maur, Karin Von. The Sound of Painting: Music in Modern Art. New York: Prestel-Verlag, 1999.

Neuenschwander, Brody. Letterwork: Creative Letterforms in Graphic Design. London: Phaidon Press Ltd, 1993.

O'Reighan, Vulva, ed. Vaughan Oliver. Vaughan Oliver and V 23 Graphic Works 1988–94. Gingko Press, 1997.

Pesch, Martin, and Markus Weisbeck. Techno Style. Germany: Edition Olms, 1998.

Poyner, Rick. Typography Now Two: Implosion. Hearst Books, 1998.

Reynolds, Simon. Blissed Out: The Raptures of Rock. Serpent's Tail, 1990.

Shaughnessy, Adrian. Sampler: Contemporary Music Graphics. London: Laurence King, 1999.

Tomato. Process: A Tomato Project. London: Thames & Hudson Ltd, 1996.

Tufte, Edward. Visual Explanations: Images and Quantities, Evidence and Narrative. New Haven: Graphics Press, 1997.

————. The Visual Display of Quantitative Information. New Haven: Graphics Press, 1992.

————. Envisioning Information. New Haven: Graphics Press, 1990.

VanderLans, Rudy. Emigre: Graphic Design into the Digital Realm. John Wiley & Sons, 1997.

Walton, Roger. Typographics 2 Cybertype: Zines + Screens. North Light Books, 1998.

————. Sight for Sound: Design + Music Mixes. Hearst Books, 1997.

Woolman, Matt, and Jeff Bellantoni. Moving Type: Designing for Time and Space. Crans, Switzerland: RotoVision, SA, 2000.

————. Type in Motion: Innovations in Digital Graphics. London: Thames & Hudson Ltd, New York: Rizzoli, 1999.

Wozencroft, Jon. The Graphic Language of Neville Brody 2. London: Thames & Hudson Ltd, 1994.

————. The Graphic Language of Neville Brody. London: Thames & Hudson Ltd, 1988.

GLOSSARY

This is an alphabetical list of terms used in the text that may need further clarification. Additional definitions are listed as they apply to music and/or image.

ACCENT: relative prominence of an element by greater intensity of variation, or modulation of pitch or tone.

ACOUSTIC: of, relating to, or being an instrument that does not feature electronically modified sound.

ACOUSTICS: the scientific study of sound. The total effect of sound, especially as produced in an enclosed space.

ACOUSTOPTICS: the science of the interaction of acoustic and optical phenomena.

AMBIENT: music constructed of electronically generated sounds, usually from computers and synthesizers. Also known as environmental music as it contains no recognizable structure, such as rhythm or melody.

AMPLITUDE: fullness; greatness of size; loudness.

BEAT: a regular, measured unit of time.

CACOPHONY: jarring, discordant sound; dissonance.

CADENCE: a progression of chords moving to a harmonic close or point of rest.

CENT: the unit of measuring intervals is known as a cent. There are 100 cents to a tempered semitone and 1200 to an octave.

CHORD: combination of three or more notes sounded simultaneously.

CHROMATIC SCALE: consisting of twelve notes within an octave, separated by semitones.

CONSONANCE: agreement, harmony, accord.

COUNTERPOINT: music consisting of two or more lines that sound simultaneously. The individual melodies form the horizontal element, and the intervals between them represent the vertical element.

DIATONIC SCALE: seven pitches within an octave of a major or minor key.

DIE-CUT: the shaping or cutting of products printed on cardboard, paper, card, stock or other material by applying pressure with a sharp-edged steel cutter.

DISSOLVE UNIT: an electronic device that allows scene transitions in a film or video tape to be made by fading out (or dimming) one scene, while the next scene comes into focus.

DISSONANCE: harsh, disagreeable combination of sounds; discord.

DISTORTION: an undesired change in the waveform of a signal. A consequence of such a change especially a lack of fidelity in reception or reproduction.

DURATION: continuance or persistence of time; short/sustained.

FEEDBACK: a return of a portion of the output of a process or system to its input, especially used to maintain performance or to control a system or process.

FIDELITY: the degree to which an electronic system accurately reproduces the sound or image of its input signal.

FREQUENCY: the number of complete cycles of a periodic process or vibration occurring in a specified time (often 1 second) and usually measured in Hertz.

FUNDAMENTAL: the lowest tone, such as the bass note of a chord.

HARMONY: musical tones sounded simultaneously—the chordal, or vertical, structure of a musical composition.

HISS: constant interference; a sharp, sibilant sound similar to a sustained "s."

IMPROVISATION: to invent, compose, recite without preparation.

INDETERMINATE: not precisely fixed; not leading to a definite result or ending.

INTERVAL: space/time between two points; difference in pitch between two tones.

INVERSION: substitution of higher for lower tones, and vice versa.

JUST INTONATION: a system of tuning based on notes whose frequencies are related by ratios of small integers.

KEY: on a keyboard, the part that is depressed by the performer's fingers to produce a sound. The main note or tonal center of a composition to which all notes are related.

LEGATO: in a smooth, even style; to tie or bind together.

MATERIAL: concerned with the physical as distinct from the intellectual, spiritual or aural. The substance out of which a thing is or can be made.

MEASURE: a group of beats—units of musical time—the first of which usually has an accent. These groups occur in numbers of two, three, four, five or more and are separated from one another by vertical bar lines.

MELODY: a path of musical tones; a complex line/path, or plane (as opposed to harmony, which is a collection of musical tones sounded simultaneously). Melody and harmony represent the horizontal and vertical elementsof musical texture, which is directly linked to rhythm.

METER: the pattern of fixed temporal units called beats, by which the rhythm of a particular musical composition is measured.

MIDI: an acronym for Musical Instrument Digital Interface, which is the standard term in the music industry for digital instrument creation and communication.

MODULATION: change of key within a composition.

NOTATION: the method(s) used to visualize music, similar to the employment of typographic letterforms to visualize the spoken word.

OCTAVE: the range of eight notes in the diatonic scale, where the eighth note has twice the frequency of the first.

OSTINATO: a short melody or phrase that is constantly repeated, usually at the same pitch.

OVERLAY CELLS: transparencies that are layered to create animated scenes.

PHRASE: a section of the musical line, similar to a written phrase.

PITCH: location of a musical sound in the tonal scale as determined by frequency.

POLYRHYTHM: two rhythmic patterns in a single structure; simultaneous, contrasting rhythms.

REST: pause; silence between notes.

RETROGRADE: a melody read backward: last note first, first note last.

RHYTHM: the pattern formed by a series of notes of differing duration and stress.

SAMPLING: an electronic technique in contemporary musical practice that is closely identified with hip-hop, sampling captures a sound segment from any source for the purpose of using it as a musical element.

SCALE: tonal sequence arranged in the order of either ascending or descending pitches.

STACCATO: cut short crisply; disconnected, abrupt.

STAVE (staff): a series of horizontal lines, totaling five in conventional musical notation, on which notes are placed. The position of the notes on the stave give a visual reference to their pitch.

STATIC: variable interference; obstruction.

SYNCOPATION: a shift of accent in a passage or composition that occurs when a normally weak beat is stressed.

SYNESTHESIA: a condition in which one type of stimulation evokes the sensation of another, i.e., hearing sound produces the visualization of a color.

SYNTHESIZER: an electronic device used to artificially create pitches and timbres.

TEMPO: the speed of a musical composition or a section of it, ranging from very slow to very fast.

TIMBRE: the quality of a sound that distinguishes it from other sounds of the same pitch and volume.

TONE: a sound of distinct pitch, quality and duration; an interval comprising two semitones.

VOICE: a distinctive style, manner or medium of expression.

WAVELENGTH: the distance between one peak of a wave of light or sound, and the next peak.

CREDITS

WHY NOT ASSOCIATES, pp 052–055
Commissioned by Nancy Berry, Vice Chairman of Virgin Records Worldwide • Produced by Caroline True • Post-production: Clear

EIKES GRAFISCHER HORT, pp 58–65
Summer Event, 1999 • Poster • Client: Helium, Frankfurt • Art direction/design: Eike Koenig

Orbit Records, 1999 • Print advertising • Art direction/design: Eike Koenig • Photography: Eike Koenig, Achim Reichert

Tyrell Corp., 2000 • Vinyl cover • Client: Polydor Zeitgeist/Universal Music • Art direction/design: Eike Koenig, Ralf Hiemisch

Diver + Ace, 1999 • Vinyl cover • Client: Orbit Records/Virgin Records • Art direction: Eike Koenig, Ralf Hiemisch • Sketch 1: Eike Koenig, Ralf Hiemisch • Sketch 2: Achim Reichert

Oliver Lieb, 1999 • Vinyl cover • Client: Orbit Records/Virgin Records • Art direction/design: Eike Koenig, Ralf Hiemisch • 3-D illustration: Ralf Hiemisch

Celvin Rotane, 1999 • Vinyl cover • Client: Orbit Records/Virgin Records • Art direction/design: Eike Koenig, Ralf Hiemisch • Set design: Ralf Hiemisch • Photography: Eike Koenig

Gouryella, 1998 • Vinyl cover • Client: Orbit Records/Virgin Records • Art direction/design: Eike Koenig, Ralf Hiemisch • Illustration: Ralf Hiemisch

Fridge, 1999 • Vinyl cover • Client: Orbit Records/ Virgin Records • Art direction/design: Eike Koenig, Ralf Hiemisch

Dune & the London Session Orchestra, 1998 • Cover and inside pages of booklet • Client: Orbit Records/Virgin Records • Art direction/design: Eike Koenig, Ralf Hiemisch • Photography: Gaby Gerster

KayCee • Vinyl cover • Client: Orbit Records/ Virgin Records • Art direction/design: Eike Koenig, Ralf Hiemisch • Photography: Eike Koenig

Marc et Claude, 1998 • Vinyl cover, promotional poster • Client: Orbit Records/Virgin Records • Art direction/design: Eike Koenig

Marc et Claude, 1999 • Vinyl cover • Client: Orbit Records/Virgin Records • Art direction/design: Eike Koenig, Ralf Hiemisch • 3-D illustration: Ralf Hiemisch • Photography: Eike Koenig

STUDIO DUMBAR, pp 066–071
North Sea Jazz poster, 1999 • Design: Maarten Jurriaanse/Miek Walda • Photography: Peter Leurink • Client: North Sea Jazz BV, The Hague

North Sea Jazz poster, 1999 • Design: Mónica Peón • Client: North Sea Jazz BV, The Hague

De kardinale Deugden poster series, 1999 • Design: Mónica Peón/Bob van Dijk • Client: Zeebelt Theatre, The Hague

Holland Dance Festival posters, 1995 and 1998 • Design: Bob van Dijk • Photography: Deen van Meer • Client: Holland Dance Festival

BÜRODESTRUCT, pp 88–95
Tech Itch/Decoder and Grooverider/Fabio/ Addiction, 1998 • Drum'n'bass clubnight flyers and posters • Client: Reitschule Bern • Design: Lopetz

Big Berne Beats,1998 • Clubnight flyer • Client: Rote Fabrik Zürich • Design: Lopetz

Neotropic, 1997 • Concert flyer and poster • Client: Reitschule Bern • Design: Lopetz

Schaltkreis, 1999 • Clubnight flyer • Client: Gaskessel Bern • Design: H1reber

Future Loop Foundation, 1998 • Concert flyer and poster • Client: Reitschule Bern • Design: Lopetz

Holy Moments, 2000 • Promotional postcard for BüroDestruct • Photography: MBrunner

Mouse on Mars, 1998 • Concert flyer and poster • Client: Reitschule Bern • Design: Lopetz

Clear, 1997 • Labelnight flyer and poster • Client: Reitschule Bern • Design: Lopetz

Clear, 1996 • Drum'n'bass clubnight flyer and poster • Client: United Tribes Bern • Design: Lopetz

David Holmes, 1998 • Concert flyer and poster • Client: Reitschule Bern • Design: Lopetz

Ed Rush/Trace, 1998 • Drum'n'bass clubnight flyer and poster • Client: Reitschule Bern • Design: Lopetz

Mark Broom, 1998 • Concert flyer and poster • Client: Reitschule Bern • Design: H1reber

Lemon D/dillinja, 1999 • Drum'n'bass clubnight flyer and poster • Client: Reitschule Bern • Design: Lopetz

Fluke, 1997 • Concert flyer and poster • Client: Wasserwerk Bern • Design: Lopetz

Alex Reece, 1997 • Concert flyer and poster • Client: Wasserwerk Bern • Design: H1reber/Lopetz

Jimi Tenor, 1997 • Concert flyer and poster • Client: Rote Fabrik Zürich • Design: H1reber/Lopetz

Peshay, 1999 • Drum'n'bass clubnight flyer and poster • Client: Reitschule Bern • Design: Lopetz

Büro Discotec, 2000 • BüroDestruct clubnight flyer and poster

Sun Electric, 1997 • Concert flyer and poster • Client: Reitschule Bern • Design: Lopetz

Randall + Storm, 1998 • Drum'n'bass clubnight flyer and poster • Client: Reitschule Bern • Design: Lopetz

BAM, pp 104–05
1999 Next Wave and 2000 Spring Concert • Concept and brochure design: Jason Ring • All other materials designed by Tifenn Aubert, James Harley and Jason Ring

STEFAN SAGMEISTER, pp 106–11
Pro-Pain, 1994 • Client: Energy Records • Art direction: Stefan Sagmeister • Design: Stefan Sagmeister, Veronica Oh • Photography: Jeffrey Silverthorne

Afropea 3, 1995 • Client: Warner Bros. Music Inc./Luaka Bop • Art direction: Stefan Sagmeister • Design: Stefan Sagmeister, Veronica Oh • Photography: Tom Schierltz • Illustration: Indigo Arts

Pat Metheny Group, 1997 • Client: Warner Jazz • Design: Stefan Sagmeister, Hajalti Karlsson • Computer work: Mathias Kern • Photography: Tom Schierltz/Stock

David Byrne, 1997 • Client: Warner Bros. Music Inc./Luaka Bop • Art direction: Stefan Sagmeister, David Byrne • Design: Stefan Sagmeister, Hjalti Karlsson • Models: Yuji Yoshimoto

H.P. Zinker, 1994 • Client: Energy Records • Art direction: Stefan Sagmeister • Design: Stefan Sagmeister, Veronica Oh • Photography: Tom Schierlitz

Skeleton Key, 1997 • Client: Capitol Records • Art direction: Stefan Sagmeister • Design: Stefan Sagmeister, Hjalti Karlsson • Photography: Tom Schierlitz

SECOND STORY pp 158–61
Forest for the Trees website • Producers: Justin Landskron and Adam Sommers, DreamWorks Records • Site design: Second Story • Sound/design: Julie Beeler • Art direction/design: Brad Johnson • Code/design: Ken Mitsumoto

Book Design: -IZATION • Typeface: DIN Neuzeit Grotesk Light & Bold Condensed • Title-page photo: David Steadman • Contents page and endpapers (front): electron microscope image of a vinyl record • Section openers, designed by Angeline Robertson: detail of player-piano music roll, electron microscope image of a vinyl record and electron microscope image of a CD • Endpapers (back): electron microscope image of a CD

INDEX / WEBSITES